# BEVERLEY PIPER'S
## QUICK & EASY
# HEALTHY
## COOKERY

BBC BOOKS

Published by BBC Books, a division of
BBC Enterprises Limited, Woodlands,
80 Wood Lane, London W12 0TT

First published 1992
© Beverley Piper 1992

ISBN 0 563 36339 8
Designed by Peter Bridgewater
Photographs by James Murphy
Styling by Jane McLish
Home Economist Allyson Birch
Nutritionist Anita Bean

Set in Bembo by Redwood Press Ltd
Printed and bound in Great Britain by
Clays Ltd, St Ives Plc
Colour separations by Tecknik Ltd,
Berkhamstead
Cover printed by Clays Ltd, St Ives Plc

## About the author

Since appearing on BBC Television's *Pebble Mill at One*, demonstrating healthy microwave cooking and producing a number of successful books on the subject, Beverley Piper's name has become synonymous with healthy cookery.

A qualified home economist and cookery teacher, Beverley now runs her own business, Creative Food Services. She also contributes articles to magazines, compiles cookery leaflets for major food companies and regularly demonstrates cookery at exhibitions. Her main interests revolve around healthy eating and promoting the quick, easy, cost–effective and varied aspects of healthy food.

Beverley lives in Ashford in Kent and has two grown–up sons.

## Acknowledgements

I would like to thank Heather Holden-Brown at BBC Books for giving me the pleasure and enjoyment in writing this book. Thanks must also go to Tina Dorman for her dedicated support in typing the manuscript and to Malcolm and Adam for tasting so many new recipes, always with some degree of enthusiasm!

## BBC BOOKS · Quick and Easy Cookery Series

Launched in 1989 by Ken Hom and Sarah Brown, the *Quick and Easy Cookery* series is a culinary winner. Everything about the titles is aimed at quick and easy recipes – the store-cupboard introductions, the ingredients and cooking methods, the menu section at the back of the books. Eight pages of colour photographs are also included to provide a flash of inspiration for the frantic or faint-hearted.

OTHER TITLES IN THE SERIES: Ken Hom's Quick and Easy Chinese Cookery • Sarah Brown's Quick and Easy Vegetarian Cookery • Clare Connery's Quick and Easy Salads • Joanna Farrow's Quick and Easy Fish Cookery • Sandeep Chatterjee's Quick and Easy Indian Vegetarian Cookery. • All at £5.99.

# CONTENTS

# INTRODUCTION

Perhaps, like me, you lead a pretty frantic life, trying to juggle too many things on a daily basis, and yet you feel fairly strongly about feeding your friends and family healthily. This book, carefully worked on with you in mind, provides quick and easy-to-follow recipes, compiled in a healthy and fun way.

People are now aware that to keep young and energetic we do need to follow a reasonably healthy diet and life-style. Most of us should cut down on some foods, such as animal fats and sugar, whilst increasing our intake of the fibre-rich, starchy foods like bread, pasta and rice, fruit and vegetables.

You will find these recipes do just that and they are all straightforward to shop for. You should be able to find all the ingredients in any large supermarket – I think this is very important as there is nothing worse than shopping in a bit of a hurry and finding that one or two of them are not stocked in that particular store.

To make life easy, several of the recipes use convenience products such as packet, canned or frozen foods so you will frequently find that the majority of ingredients are close at hand anyway. Most convenience foods are nutritionally sound, they're easy to store and quick to use.

The book is divided into chapters, set out like any conventional cookery book. Each quick and easy recipe starts with an introduction giving a few interesting and nutritional facts and serving suggestions, where appropriate. Healthy eating is considered not only in the recipe itself but also in any accompanying vegetables, sauces etc.

'Speedy Starters' offer interesting recipes which are ideal for many occasions. You may like to pick two or three of them to serve as a main meal or indeed combine one with a recipe from the vegetable section. Try Cheesey Rice Tomatoes (see p. 24) from the starter section with Crunchy Vegetable Stir-Fry (see p. 47) from the vegetable section for a quick lunch. The starters include quick soups, pâtés and healthy vegetable dishes, many of which require hardly any, if any cooking at all.

'Super-Fast Fish' includes a lot of my favourite recipes with interesting variations on preparing fish that are a bit different. Various cooking methods are used and as all the recipes, except the Sardine Toasties (see p. 38), are designed to be served as main meals, I have suggested accompaniments. Try Salmon Savoury (see p. 30) and Tangy Halibut (see p. 43) which is cooked on a bed of sliced citrus fruits and has a lovely fresh, fruity flavour.

'Vegetables and Instant Salad Dishes' show quick ways of presenting high fibre vegetables differently. The salads use raw ingredients, and not too many of them, so this section is particularly quick and the finished recipes are colourful and look stunning on the serving dish.

'Quick Main Meals' and 'Rapid Rice and Pasta Meals' both cover dishes which are mostly complete in themselves, or perhaps need just a salad and some bread to accompany them.

You'll find that throughout the book preparation is straightforward, as quick as possible and you won't have too many pans to wash up afterwards either!

'Perfect Poultry' is a chapter of new ideas, plus some old favourites for chicken, duck, turkey and chicken livers and the meat and bacon recipes use healthy cuts made quickly into tasty main meals. My family love the Chilli Turkey (see p. 105) and the Easy Coq au Vin (see p. 111).

The last chapter offers a varied selection of healthy, quick desserts as well as some original ideas for instant puddings. Also included are one or two baking recipes which I am sure will be popular.

At the end of the book you will find a selection of daily menus for different occasions using various recipes from the book. Each menu serves four people and will help you plan several days of quick and easy healthy eating at a glance.

Above all I hope you will enjoy, even half as much as I did, making these quick and easy healthy recipes and serving them to family and friends.

# NOTES ON THE RECIPES

• All recipes serve four unless otherwise indicated.
• All eggs are size 3.
• British standard measuring spoons, level, have been used throughout.
• Follow one set of measurements only. Don't mix imperial and metric.
• Throughout the book, measurements of yoghurt and fromage frais are given in ml (fl oz) but both are sold in cartons labelled in grammes.

   1 small pot of yoghurt 150 ml (5 fl oz) is 50 g.

   1 large pot yoghurt or fromage frais is 500 g and marked only as such.
• Where cartons, packets and tins are used, sizes printed on the actual products are given. Use the nearest size available to you.

# THE STORE-CUPBOARD
# AND HEALTHY FOODS

If you organise your food storage areas, store-cupboard, refrigerator, vegetable rack and freezer to house most of the following foods on a regular basis, you will find it particularly easy to put the recipes in this book together quickly. You will also be well on the way to following a healthy eating life-style if you make sure that these staples gradually take over from less healthy ingredients.

### STORE-CUPBOARD

Rice: particularly brown rice, wild rice, easy cook rice • Pasta: several varieties and shapes, including one wholegrain variety, and one with spinach • Cereals: breakfast cereals without added sugar, wheat flakes and porridge oats as well as one crunchy breakfast cereal with dried fruits • Flour: wholemeal plain and self-raising, plain flour, cornflour • Savoury spread such as yeast extract • Cans of pulse vegetables: red kidney beans, chick peas, haricot beans, baked beans • Cans of fruit in natural juice: three varieties • Cans of low fat, evaporated milk • Dried fruits: raisins, sultanas, dried apricots, fruit salad • Cans of fish: tuna, sardines, salmon, crab, all canned in water or brine • Cans of vegetables: without added salt or sugar – bean sprouts, sweetcorn, chopped tomatoes • Oil: sunflower, walnut and olive oil • Juices: cartons of pure orange juice • Herbs: a selection of dried herbs, but do grow fresh herbs on the kitchen window-sill if at all possible • Lemon juice • Vinegar: white wine and raspberry • Nuts: almonds, walnuts, cashew nuts, pecan • Jams: low sugar fruit conserves, three varieties • Soy sauce • Stock cubes, reduced salt if possible • Lentils • Honey • Brown sugar

### REFRIGERATOR

Reduced fat Cheddar type cheese • Cottage cheese • Edam cheese • Eggs • Fromage frais • Reduced fat cream cheese • Curd cheese • Yoghurt • Polyunsaturated margarine and low fat spread ♦ Semi–skimmed milk ♦ Tomato purée ♦ Tomato juice ♦ Apple juice ♦ Reduced calorie mayonnaise ♦Lean bacon and ham

**FREEZER**

White and oily fish: two or three varieties of each, plus shelled prawns ♦ Chicken: different cuts as well as whole chickens ♦ Turkey breasts ♦ Vegetables: peas, sweetcorn, spinach, mixed vegetables ♦ Fruits: Bramley apples, raspberries and redcurrants ♦ Wholemeal bread

**FRESH PRODUCE**

Wholemeal bread ♦ Fruit in season, including lemons and limes ♦ Vegetables in season ♦ Ginger ♦ Garlic ♦ Herbs: a variety on the window-sill ♦ Lean cuts of meat ♦ Fresh fish, oily and white ♦ Salad ingredients

# HEALTHY FOODS

**FISH**

A fresh food that is as quick to cook as any 'convenience' food.

Fish forms a very important part of a healthy diet. Both white fish, which has only 20 calories per ounce, and oily fish, with only 55 calories per ounce, are high in body building protein and rich in B vitamins.

Oily fish provides vitamin A for healthy eyes, skin and hair and vitamin D which is essential for healthy bones and teeth. Fish is also an important source of iodine, fluorine and calcium (in the bones), minerals needed for the body's growth and metabolism. The fat present in oily fish (white fish contains only traces of fat in the liver) is polyunsaturated – the type of fat recommended by the medical profession for a healthy heart. White fish is particularly easy to digest.

**MEAT AND POULTRY**

Meat, including bacon, is an excellent source of protein, minerals and vitamins and only a small amount provides most of the nutrients we need for a healthy diet. All meat contains fat, and offal, such as liver and kidneys, has a fairly high cholesterol level and should therefore only be served once a week. Use less meat in recipes, extending it with rice, pasta, vegetables and pulses to make appetising, healthy meals. Chicken and turkey provide economical lean meat. Use both in imaginative ways. Turkey mince is now available frozen and may be cooked straight from the freezer.

## DAIRY FOODS

Switch from high fat dairy foods such as butter and double cream to reduced fat alternatives. Use semi-skimmed milk which provides all the B vitamins and calcium found in whole milk but almost half the fat. Buy fromage frais and low fat yoghurt instead of cream to serve with desserts. Use quark low fat soft cheese instead of cream cheese in pâtés, spreads and cheese-cakes. Avoid hard cheeses like Cheddar, Lancashire and Cheshire. Use Parmesan for flavouring and Edam, Brie and Camembert for ploughmans, sandwiches etc. Make friends with cottage cheese, mixing it with chopped chives, herbs or minced onion for added flavour.

Remember, however, that hard matured Cheddar has a wonderful flavour in cooking and a little goes a long way so don't feel too worried about using it in soufflés, sauces, gratinée dishes, cheese scones etc, but do try the new reduced fat Cheddar type cheese as well. Low fat spreads are now readily available as alternatives to butter and margarine. Many are excellent in baking too. Ensure that the spread you buy is labelled 'high in polyunsaturates'. Select cooking oils that are high in polyunsaturates. They are quick and easy to mix in, so use them in biscuits, cakes, scones and in crumble toppings.

## QUORN

Quorn is a delicious wholesome new food. It is vegetable in origin, low in fat, and a good source of dietary fibre and protein, containing no cholesterol. Quorn makes an excellent alternative to meat as it has the texture of lean meat yet is grown from a tiny relative of the mushroom. Ounce for ounce it contains as much protein as an egg and as much dietary fibre as fresh green vegetables, yet it is low in calories.

Quorn is bought pre-cooked so simply requires heating through and can be ready in 4–5 minutes. It picks up the flavours from the ingredients it's cooked with such as onions, garlic, tomatoes, wine and lemon juice so use about half the usual amount of these flavourings.

Quorn is readily available in your supermarket. Look in the chill cabinet for the pack with the green and yellow stripes. Try it in casseroles, stir-fry recipes and try grilling or currying it. Quorn freezes successfully and will keep in the freezer for up to three months.

## EGGS

Eggs are the most complete single source of protein available. They also provide calcium and phosphorus for strong bones and healthy, strong teeth, and iron, which helps prevent anaemia.

Fat soluble vitamins, A and D, are in the yolk plus B vitamins for healthy skin and nerves. Although eggs do contain cholesterol it is now considered fine to include them in your diet as long as you don't over-indulge. 3–4 eggs per week is fine provided that your doctor has not advised otherwise.

For quick and easy meals eggs are fabulous. They can be scrambled with tomatoes and prawns for a tasty supper dish, poached and served with kippers for a speedy lunch and hard-boiled to add to kedgeree and salads. They are excellent as a binding ingredient and can be added to sauces and used as a topping over dishes like cauliflower cheese and lasagne.

## VEGETABLES – FRESH AND FROZEN

Vegetables are a valuable source of fibre and vitamins, particularly A and C. They are also known to act as a preventative for some cancers. Above all they're super-quick to prepare and cook and excellent used raw in salads etc.

*Keeping vegetables* Fresh vegetables do not keep well and those that contain vitamin C are particularly vulnerable as it is quickly lost. Buy in small quantities and use them as soon as possible. Carrots, parsnips, swedes and onions will keep for up to 10 days in a cool well-ventilated vegetable rack.

Frozen vegetables are superb convenience foods and although not as good as fresh vegetables, still have excellent food value.

*Cooking vegetables* Don't peel vegetables unless it's really necessary as there are fibre and vitamins in the skin. A quick scrub under the cold tap is quite sufficient. Cut them into even pieces and cook in a saucepan with a tightly fitting lid. Use a minimum amount of water and avoid salt. Cook until tender-crisp – overcooked vegetables are definitely out of fashion. Use the cooking water to make a sauce or gravy. Vegetables are also excellent steamed, stir-fried or cooked in the microwave.

## SALAD VEGETABLES

Buy little and often and keep refrigerated in a plastic bag. Wash well before using and tear leaves into bite-size pieces with your hands. Prepare and serve salads as soon as possible. Adding chopped fresh herbs to salad will give it a wonderful fresh flavour. Two or three salad ingredients in a bowl is quite sufficient for a tasty side dish, but choose a variety of colours and textures.

## HERBS

Fresh herbs will grow happily on the window-sill and are wonderful in cookery. Use them to liven up salad and vegetable dishes. They can be added to butter or polyunsaturated margarine, frozen and used straight from the freezer to transform hot vegetables. They are also useful in garlic bread, delicious in omelettes, soups, sauces and stuffings and wonderful in salad dressings.

Try basil on tomatoes and green salads and chervil in rice salads. Chives go well with egg, potato and cheese dishes and are super-quick to snip with scissors.

Coriander and parsley are great favourites as a garnish if you use the whole leaf, as is mint, and, if you have all three, see what a difference they make, finely chopped in the next mixed salad you prepare, particularly if you've used some fresh fruit with the salad leaves. Crushed frozen parsley can be added as an ingredient to stews, casseroles, soups etc. Always use fresh parsley as a garnish. To chop fresh parsley quickly, put the sprigs into a mug and chop them with a pair of scissors.

### DRIED HERBS

Dried herbs, as long as they are really fresh (lift the lid and you'll soon know as dried herbs past their best smell horribly musty), are a wonderful stand-by in the kitchen. They are ready chopped and can be used both in making up a recipe and for sprinkling over the dish once it is complete.

Buy in small quantities and keep two or three varieties in stock. As a rough guide, use dried herbs in any recipe which suggests fresh herbs – just halve the amount stipulated.

### GARLIC

Our ancestors believed garlic to have very special medical properties. Indeed it was the most widely used medicinal plant in the world. Garlic has an antibacterial effect and is therefore excellent for sore throats. It also helps indigestion sufferers and is now known to aid the elimination of cholesterol from the body.

Garlic also adds flavour to many foods. Don't worry too much about bad breath, I find that fresh garlic lessens the smell. It can also soon be cured by eating a sprig of fresh parsley. Garlic in frozen dishes does seem to cause problems, in which case it is a good idea to use a fresh breath spray, readily available from chemists and most supermarkets.

### BREAD

Although all bread is nutritionally a good food to eat, it is well worth swopping to wholemeal varieties, the most obvious advantage being that it's far higher in fibre. Two slices from a large wholemeal loaf provides 5.6 g (approximately ¼ oz) of fibre whilst two slices from a large white loaf provides almost zero fibre so there is quite a difference. One thick slice of wholemeal bread also provides 44 per cent of the recommended daily amount of vitamin B1 (thiamine), 32 per cent of calcium and 33 per cent of the daily iron recommended and, at just 95 calories per slice, it does show you just how nutritionally valuable wholemeal bread is.

### FROMAGE FRAIS

This low fat soft cheese from France is my idea of heaven! It has a light texture and creamy taste and is ideal as a replacement for cream, full fat cream cheese or mayonnaise in lots of recipes both sweet and savoury. You will find it used in various ways in a number of recipes in this book. Buy it in plastic tubs in the supermarket, usually stored near the yoghurt. Fromage frais contains only 108 calories per 100 g ( 4 oz) with 7.2 g (approximately $^{1}/_{8}$ oz) of fat of which only 4.4 g ($^{1}/_{16}$ oz) are saturated.

# WHY EAT HEALTHILY?

In 1983, the National Advisory Committee of Nutritional Information blew the whistle on the British diet, emphasising that other countries, particularly those in the Mediterranean, suffered far fewer dietary related diseases such as heart attacks and strokes and had substantially lower cancer statistics than those in Britain. Similarly, the Eskimos and Japanese have a very low incidence of heart disease. Unfortunately, the UK has one of the highest instances of heart disease in the world. Somewhat alarmingly, 27 per cent of deaths in the UK in 1988 were due to heart disease.

In the healthier Mediterranean countries the food is rich in olive oil and garlic and the people eat large amounts of fish, fruit and vegetables, bread, salads, pasta and rice dishes, and far less refined foods and red meat than the British.

About one-third of our adult population is overweight and if you are a little on the portly side, there are several health disadvantages. You are far more likely to suffer heart disease, have back trouble, gallstones, high blood pressure, varicose veins, diabetes, strokes etc. It's therefore well worth working at a healthy diet because by changing your diet to a more healthy one the pounds will naturally roll away.

## WHAT ELSE CAN WE DO?

• Take more exercise. A 40-minute brisk walk, every day, will give you a feeling of well-being, reduce stress, tone up the muscles, including your heart, and help you lose weight.

• Cut down on alcohol. Alcohol is full of empty calories. If you like a drink, try white wine topped up with soda water and served with ice for a refreshing spritzer. This is a long drink and is a better option health-wise.

• Don't add salt in cooking, or at the table. Salt is present in virtually every processed food we buy, be it a packet of biscuits or a can of baked beans. By reducing your salt intake you really do reduce your likelihood of suffering from a stroke.

• Eat more fibre foods. Unpeeled vegetables, peas, beans, sweetcorn and canned pulses such as red kidney beans are particularly good for you. Eat plenty of fruits, particularly bananas and raspberries, and wholemeal bread; pasta and high fibre breakfast cereals.

• Reduce your intake of high fat protein foods. Although protein is needed for growth and good health, we simply do not need the usual amount consumed in British households.

• Avoid pre-cooked convenience foods like pies, pasties, quiches, cakes, biscuits, chocolate, crisps and salted peanuts. You'll be cutting down on fat, salt and sugar. Buy fruit, natural yoghurt and wholemeal bread instead.

• Check labels on packets and cans and buy those with the least amount of fat, salt and sugar.

• Don't think fat, think polyunsaturated. Fat is necessary in our diets as it is a wonderful source of energy, fat-soluble vitamins and essential fatty acids and is needed to cushion the organs in our bodies, such as the liver and kidneys. However, fat is found, in varying amounts, in practically every food we eat so it is not difficult to meet our requirements. It is high in calories so it is far better to reduce fat intake where possible. The recipes in this book do just that and although fat is mentioned in the healthy content, if it occurs in the recipe, you will find that all the recipes have been carefully compiled to be low in fat and to use polyunsaturated fats instead of hard animal fats.

• Give up or at least cut down on smoking. You'll be far less likely to suffer a heart attack. Whenever you crave for a cigarette try eating an orange instead. It really did help me when I gave it up. In the UK twelve people die every hour from smoking-related diseases. Make sure you are not one of them.

# COOKING METHODS

The way food is cooked affects the amount of fat actually retained in the food so microwave, steam or grill instead of frying, although stir-frying, with a little polyunsaturated oil, is excellent for quick healthy eating. Remove the skin from poultry before you cook it and if you are using mince, dry fry it and drain off the fat residue before you continue with the method.

## THE MICROWAVE OVEN
## AND HEALTHY EATING

If you are fortunate enough to own a microwave, use it. It's a boon for the healthy eater, being quick, clean and efficient.

• Fish and vegetables can be cooked in the minimum of liquid for taste, maximum nutritional value and speed. Cook straight from frozen if you wish.

• De-frosting is quick and efficient so a nutritious meal can be prepared from the freezer in super-quick time.

• The microwave re-heats food, even pasta and rice, with no loss of nutrients or drying out. Make sure you cover the food and stir once or twice for even heating.

• Prepare stewed fruit in the microwave from fresh or frozen fruit without adding liquid so the fruit tastes really fresh and fruity. Leave to stand for a while and then stir in a little sugar.

### STOCK

Home-made stock is the ideal base for several of the quick and easy recipes in this book, although a cube can be used if you're pushed for time. Try and find a reduced salt variety – it's probably worth buying a selection next time you're in a health food shop.

*Microwave stock* Stock may be made quickly and efficiently in the microwave, with few smells left lingering in the kitchen.

*Fish stock.* Put roughly 1 kg (2 lb) fish heads, bones, skin etc, into a 3 litre (5–6 pint) casserole dish. Cover with water. Add 2 or 3 sprigs of fresh herbs and 1 sliced onion. Cover and bring to boiling point on full power. Then cook for 10 minutes on defrost. Allow to cool, then strain.

*Vegetable stock.* Put 450 g (1 lb) freshly prepared mixed vegetables such as carrots, swedes, turnips, onions and celery (or the equivalent in frozen vegetables) into a 3 litre (5–6 pint) bowl. Add 2 teaspoons dried mixed herbs with a few peppercorns and a small can of chopped tomatoes. Cover with water and a lid and bring to boiling point on full power. Then cook for 20 minutes on defrost. Allow to cool, then strain.

*Chicken stock.* Put the split carcass and giblets from the chicken into a 3 litre (5–6 pint) bowl. Add a bay leaf and 2 teaspoons dried mixed herbs with 2 chopped onions and a celery stalk, chopped. Cover with water and a lid. Bring to the boil on full power and then cook for 30 minutes on defrost. Allow to cool, then strain, and skim off any fat.

***Frozen stock*** Freeze home-made stock in ice-cube trays. Bag up and label clearly. Frozen in this way the cubes will defrost quickly to be used in soups and sauces.

### FOR QUICKER COOKING

Throughout the book I have used various methods to speed up things in the kitchen; using fewer ingredients, making good use of equipment such as food processors and microwave ovens and selecting quick to cook cuts of meat, poultry etc. Bear in mind these few points which really will help you to prepare healthy food quickly and easily:

• Read through the recipes, plan the meal and shop for the necessary ingredients in good time.

• Fill dirty pans with cold water immediately after they've been used and discipline yourself to wash up as you go along.

• Make good use of time-saving equipment such as mechanical choppers, food processors, microwave ovens, electric mixers etc.

# S P E E D Y  S T A R T E R S

**P**eople in a hurry often think they haven't the time to prepare a starter, but you will find plenty of quick and easy recipes in this chapter to change that. Some of them can be prepared well in advance so won't really add to the work load of preparing a quick meal.

Starters are more than just dishes served as a first course. Two or three light imaginative starters are quite adequate as a meal in themselves and they are also great on a buffet table.

A quick bowl of hot, home-made soup is welcome at almost any time of year but especially in the winter months. Soup can quickly be extended to a main meal with the addition of bread with pâté, cheese or fresh fruit. It also re-heats well too.

Have fun creating these healthy starters which are speedy to prepare and cook – a few need no cooking at all. What could be more quick and easy than Creamy Cannellini Pâté (see p. 19) made with canned cannellini beans with vegetable oil and curry powder. Grapefruit has a wonderful flavour combined with the chicken in the Oriental Chicken Cocktail (see p. 20) and the Five-Minute Chicken Broth (see p. 21) is colourful and tastes delicious, yet cooks super-fast.

Use the 'Instant Starters' when you need a quick idea. After all, a starter really does make a meal into an occasion and these healthy versions won't give your guests that bloated feeling before the main course even arrives!

## I NSTANT STARTERS

• Top prepared grapefruit halves with a little demerara sugar and a shaking of ground cinnamon or ginger. Pop under a pre-heated grill until the sugar melts. Serve immediately.

• Fan 4 peeled avocado halves. Sieve approximately 225 g (8 oz) raspberries to a purée. Add a little sieved icing sugar to taste and serve in a pool beside the avocado.

• Peeled melon, cubed, is wonderful in sundae dishes with a little chilled crème-de-menthe poured over on serving.

• Slices of two exotic fruits such as mango and kiwi are delicious with a little crème-de-menthe or crème fraises beside them.

• Quick cold kebabs on cocktail sticks. Try cubed Swiss Gruyère cheese with black olives, seedless grapes and stoned dates. Serve with a dressing of seasoned fromage frais.

• Fill avocado halves with canned dressed crab mixed with a little reduced calorie mayonnaise and a dash of tabasco. Remember to buy the avocados a day or two in advance and allow them to ripen in the fruit bowl.

• Flavour reduced calorie mayonnaise or fromage frais with tomato purée, freshly chopped herbs and crushed garlic to taste. Serve as a dip with 2 types of vegetable sticks.

• Serve a fillet of smoked mackerel (per person) with a spoonful of cottage cheese and a salad garnish.

• Lightly cook dwarf French beans and baby sweetcorn. Drain and toss in a vinaigrette whilst still warm. Serve cold.

• Slices of Sopocka (lean Polish sausage) with a tossed mixed salad garnish.

# CHICKEN LIVER SAVOURIES

S E R V E S

—— 4 ——

These tasty savouries can be either served as a starter on a bed of shredded lettuce or on cocktail sticks at a drinks party. They can be prepared well in advance and served cold but are also delicious warm.

*Healthy Content: The liver provides protein and iron and the bacon crisps under the grill so a lot of the fat is drained away. Bacon provides protein, vitamins and minerals and contains some fat.*

**INGREDIENTS**

*8 rashers lean streaky, unsmoked bacon, rinded*
*225 g (8 oz) chicken livers*
*1 teaspoon dried thyme*

Stretch bacon out on a chopping board, using the back of a knife. Cut each rasher in half, vertically. Divide chicken livers into 16 pieces.

Roll 1 piece of bacon round each chicken liver, leaving join on underside. Sprinkle all over with thyme.

Cook under pre-heated grill for 7–10 minutes, until crisp.

# CREAMY CANNELLINI PATE

S E R V E S

—— 4 ——

This creamy pâté tastes light and fresh with just a hint of curry. Leave the pâté to stand for a while before you serve it to allow the flavours to mingle. This pâté will keep for 1–2 days if covered and kept in the refrigerator.

Serve with carrot and celery sticks, or crackers.

*Healthy Content: Cannellini beans are an excellent source of fibre, protein, B vitamins, iron and energy giving carbohydrate. (The milk provides a little calcium.)*

**INGREDIENTS**

*1 × 430 g (15 oz) can cannellini beans*
*2 cloves garlic, peeled and crushed*
*1 teaspoon medium curry powder*
*2 teaspoons tomato purée*
*1 teaspoon lemon juice*
*2 tablespoons vegetable oil*
*A little salt*
*2–3 tablespoons semi-skimmed milk*

Drain the cannellini beans and put into a food processor with the garlic, curry powder, tomato purée, lemon juice and oil. Season with salt. Process in short bursts until blended. Add the milk and process again until smooth. Turn into a serving dish and leave for 10 minutes before serving.

# ORIENTAL CHICKEN COCKTAIL

### SERVES
### — 4 —

This starter is very pretty to look at and tastes light and refreshing. The flavours of the pink grapefruit combine well with the meaty chicken and the prawns. A low fat starter that can be served before almost any main course.

***Healthy Content:*** *Grapefruit is bursting with vitamin C and the chicken and prawns provide protein.*

Peel and segment grapefruit discarding pith and membrane and holding the fruit over a mixing bowl as you work so that you reserve any juice that drips out. Cut each segment in half and add to mixing bowl. Add the chicken, prawns, radishes and coriander. Toss lightly. Add garlic and sunflower oil. Season lightly, toss again.

Shred lettuce onto side plates, top with chicken mixture and serve immediately.

**INGREDIENTS**

2 pink grapefruit or 1
  orange and 1 grapefruit
100 g (4 oz) cooked
  chicken breast, skinned
  and chopped
150 g (5 oz) peeled
  prawns
4 radishes, sliced
1 tablespoon fresh
  coriander, chopped
1 clove garlic, peeled and
  crushed
2 tablespoons sunflower oil
A little salt and freshly
  ground black pepper

TO SERVE
Frisee or little gem lettuce
  leaves

# FIVE-MINUTE CHICKEN BROTH

### S E R V E S
### — 4 —

This Chinese style soup uses left-over chicken but you could use lean pork or ham instead, or even low fat sausages, well grilled. Serve with savoury scones or bread.

**Healthy Content:** *Plenty of fibre and vitamins in this low fat soup. The chicken provides protein and the pasta adds energy giving carbohydrate.*

Put the stock into a large pan and cover with a lid. Bring to the boil. Add the cucumber, mushrooms, cabbage or spinach with the chicken and red pepper. Stir well. Add the herbs, pasta (if desired) and a seasoning of black pepper. Cover and return to the boil.

Simmer gently for 5 minutes and serve immediately.

### INGREDIENTS

*1 litre (1 ³/₄ pints) chicken stock*
*Half a cucumber, diced*
*6 large button mushrooms, sliced*
*225 g (8 oz) spring cabbage or spinach, shredded*
*175 g (6 oz) lean cooked chicken, skinned and chopped*
*¹/₂ red pepper, de-seeded and diced*
*1 teaspoon dried mixed herbs*
*50 g (2 oz) soup pasta (optional)*
*Freshly ground black pepper*

# CRAB AND CORN CHOWDER

### SERVES

—— 4 ——

1 tablespoon olive oil
1 onion, peeled and
 chopped
2 carrots, scrubbed and
 diced
2 tablespoons plain
 wholemeal flour
450 ml (15 fl oz) chicken
 stock
450 ml (15 fl oz) semi-
 skimmed milk
275 g (10 oz) potatoes,
 scrubbed and diced
100 g (4 oz) frozen
 sweetcorn kernels
A pinch of cayenne pepper
1 × 170 g (5½ oz) can
 white crabmeat in water
 or brine, drained

TO GARNISH
2 tablespoons fresh parsley,
 chopped

Chowder originated in the USA where it was made from clams and served with warm corn biscuits as a main meal. In Britain chowder is more usually made from cod or haddock. Prawns are often added to make the soup more exciting.

Try this crab and sweetcorn version for something a little special and serve with warm granary rolls.

**Healthy Content:** *Fibre, calcium, vitamins, protein and energy-giving carbohydrate are all present in this healthy dish.*

Heat the oil in a large, heavy-based pan. Add the onion and carrot and cook over a low heat until the onion softens. This should take about 5 minutes. Stir in the flour. Gradually blend in the stock and milk. Increase the heat, stirring continuously, until the mixture boils and thickens. Add the potatoes and sweetcorn. Return to the boil, simmer for 10 minutes and remove from the heat.

Season with cayenne, add the crabmeat and stir. Sprinkle with fresh parsley and serve immediately.

# PEA AND ASPARAGUS SOUP

S E R V E S

—— 4 ——

Try this rich-tasting, creamy soup with warm granary rolls before a salad main course. Full of flavour and colour, yet made from store-cupboard ingredients, this soup is quick to make.

**Healthy Content:** *Fibre, calcium, protein, carbohydrate and very little fat. 100 g (4 oz) peas provide 45 per cent of the recommended daily intake of vitamin C and 20 per cent of the daily requirement of thiamine ($B_1$).*

Place the peas and mint into a large saucepan and add the chicken stock. Season with a little black pepper. Bring to the boil, cover and simmer gently for 5 minutes. Turn into a food processor, add the asparagus and process until smooth. Return to pan and stir in the milk. Heat thoroughly, without boiling, and stir occasionally.

Serve in individual soup bowls, garnished with a swirl of natural yoghurt and topped with a sprig of fresh mint.

**INGREDIENTS**

450 g (1 lb) frozen, minted, garden peas
4 sprigs fresh mint
600 ml (1 pint) hot chicken stock
Freshly ground black pepper
1 × 340 g (12 oz) can asparagus, drained and roughly chopped
300 ml (10 fl oz) semi-skimmed milk

**TO GARNISH**
Low fat natural yoghurt
4 sprigs fresh mint

# CHEESEY RICE TOMATOES

### SERVES
### —— 4 ——

4 large tomatoes
100 g (4 oz) brown rice,
 cooked
75 g (3 oz) Edam cheese,
 grated
1 tablespoon wholegrain
 mustard
1 teaspoon dried oregano
Freshly ground black
 pepper

Quick and easy stuffed tomatoes look attractive and taste delicious. They are surprisingly filling and an ideal starter if you serve one per person, but also make an adequate lunch if you allow two per person accompanied by a salad.

**Healthy Content:** *This recipe is high in fibre and a rich source of vitamins B and C. Energy-giving carbohydrate is provided in the rice with protein, calcium and some fat from the cheese.*

Pre-heat the oven to gas mark 4, 350°F (180°C).
 Cut 1 cm ($^1/_2$ in) off the top of each tomato. Scoop out and discard the seeds. Mix the remaining ingredients together, in a bowl, reserving a little of the cheese. Pack, tightly, into each tomato. Sprinkle remaining cheese on the top of each one and arrange on a baking dish. Bake for 15–20 minutes, until lightly golden.
 Serve immediately.

# PRAWN-STUFFED MUSHROOMS

### S E R V E S

### —— 4 ——

This quick starter contains plenty of fibre and the flavour of the mushrooms is particularly distinctive when cooked in this way. A rather special start to any meal.

**Healthy Content:** *B vitamins, plenty of fibre and protein in this recipe with calcium in the prawns. As prawns are fairly high in cholesterol they shouldn't be served more than once a week.*

---

Pre-heat the oven to gas mark 4, 350°F (180°C).

Gently remove the stalks from the mushrooms. Brush mushrooms on both sides with oil and arrange upside down on a baking sheet (or dinner plate if you have a microwave).

Chop the stalks finely and mix with the remaining ingredients. Pile the mixture onto the mushrooms and bake for 15–20 minutes or microwave on 100% full power for about 4¹/₂ minutes.

Serve immediately.

**INGREDIENTS**

*12 medium size mushrooms*
*2 tablespoons olive oil*
*3 spring onions, chopped*
*150 g (5 oz) cooked*
  *prawns, peeled and*
  *roughly chopped*
*50 g (2 oz) wholemeal*
  *breadcrumbs*
*50 g (2 oz) frozen*
  *sweetcorn kernels*
*3 teaspoons Worcestershire*
  *sauce*
*Freshly ground black*
  *pepper*

# CREAMY SALMON PATE

### SERVES

#### —— 4 ——

S almon is a versatile, delicious and healthy choice for all the family. Canned salmon is convenient to use and this soft, creamy pâté tastes so good, your guests will think you spent hours preparing it.

*Healthy Content: Salmon is high in protein, a good source of calcium and iron, provides vitamins A and D, thiamine (B₁) and riboflavin (B₂) and contains polyunsaturated fat.*

Flake the salmon into a food processor, discarding the skin and bones. Add the soft cheese, lemon juice and rind, seasoning and garlic. Process until smooth.

Turn into a shallow dish, cover and chill. Sprinkle with fresh parsley and serve with the wholemeal bread.

## INGREDIENTS

1 × 213 g (7 ¹/₂ oz) can pink or red salmon in water or brine, drained
175 g (6 oz) low fat soft cheese, with herbs
2 tablespoons lemon juice
Grated rind from ¹/₂ lemon
Freshly ground black pepper
1 clove garlic, peeled and crushed

TO SERVE
Fresh parsley, chopped
Thick slices of wholemeal cob loaf

# PRAWNS MARIE ROSE

### SERVES

#### —— 4 ——

A light refreshing starter using fresh fruit and prawns. The fromage frais adds a low fat dressing to this recipe. Those who love prawn cocktail will enjoy trying this slightly different adaptation.

*Healthy Content: Fibre, vitamins from the lettuce and peas, calcium and protein from the dressing, but prawns are fairly high in cholesterol so shouldn't be served more than once a week.*

Divide the iceberg lettuce between 4 side plates. Slice each pear half into segments and arrange in a fan on top of each plate of lettuce. Add the prawns to the side of the pears.

To make the dressing, turn the fromage frais into a mixing bowl. Add the tomato purée, parsley, garlic and seasoning and mix well.

Spoon the dressing over prawns and serve immediately.

## INGREDIENTS

Iceberg lettuce, shredded
2 ripe Williams pears, each peeled, cored and sliced in half
350 g (12 oz) cooked prawns, peeled

FOR THE DRESSING
250 ml (8 fl oz) fromage frais
1 teaspoon tomato purée
1 tablespoon fresh parsley, chopped
1 clove garlic, peeled and crushed
A little salt and freshly ground black pepper

# FRESH HERBY CORN

### S E R V E S
### — 4 —

A healthy, super-quick starter straight from the freezer. There's no preparation involved if you buy frozen corn on the cob and the flavour is delicious. Try serving the cobs with this lemon dressing instead of the usual animal fat, butter sauce.

**Healthy Content:** *Plenty of fibre, energy-giving carbohydrate and protein with vitamin C in the fresh herbs and lemon juice. Walnut oil is high in healthy polyunsaturates.*

---

Using a covered frying pan, cook the corn on the cob in a little boiling water (see directions on the packet for quantity of water) for approximately 6–8 minutes. If you are using a microwave, place cobs in a shallow dish, add 2 tablespoons cold water, cover and microwave on full power for approximately 12 minutes.

Meanwhile, prepare the dressing. Put the herbs, garlic, lemon juice and oil into a mug and season with black pepper to taste. Whisk with a fork.

Drain the cobs, pour the dressing over them and serve immediately.

## INGREDIENTS

4 frozen corn on the cob
3 tablespoons freshly
    chopped mixed herbs
**or** 2 teaspoons dried mixed
    herbs
2 cloves garlic, peeled and
    crushed
2 tablespoons lemon juice
4 tablespoons walnut oil
Freshly ground black
    pepper

## SUPER-FAST FISH

These quick, healthy and varied fish recipes prove just how quick and easy it is to include fish regularly in your diet.

Fish is one of the quickest protein-based foods to cook. It's also wonderfully versatile. Unfortunately fish remains vastly underused by British people, which is odd, considering we live on an island with an abundance of fish in the seas surrounding us.

White fish is extremely low in fat, a good source of protein and very easy to digest. Oily fish has vitamins A and D and has rich polyunsaturated oil distributed throughout its tissue. Doctors now believe it to be an invaluable food which helps to keep the blood thin and flowing freely through the arteries and thus a real asset to cardiac patients.

I've used quick, healthy methods of cooking fish such as poaching, microwaving and stir-frying and used convenience foods such as a jar of sauce in the 'Mexican Cod' (see p. 35).

Try and serve fish three times each week. Not only is it healthy and filling but it's also available fresh, in cans and frozen so make good use of it. Quick and easy healthy meals can be put together fast provided you keep a few cans of fish in the cupboard and a supply in the freezer as stand-bys.

## QUICK TIPS

• Flake any left-over fish into cold rice or pasta, add 1 drained can sweetcorn, with peppers, and toss in a vinaigrette dressing for a simple, quick salad.

• Keep a stock of frozen fish. Most fish can be cooked straight from frozen. White fish can be kept for 4 months, oily fish for 3 months and peeled prawns for up to 2 months in the freezer.

• To skin fish, dip your fingers in salt first as this makes it far easier to grip the skin. Start at the tail and rip the skin off towards the head.

• Buy convenience fish canned in brine or water for healthy eating.

• For speed, cook fish in the microwave; the flavour is also superb. Ensure you arrange it in a single layer and add a little semi-skimmed milk or stock. Cover and microwave according to your handbook. White fish, microwaved on full power, generally takes approximately 4–5 minutes for each 450 g (1 lb). Oily fish takes 5–6 minutes. (These cooking times are based on a 700 watt microwave.)

• Use herbs straight from the freezer. Crumble frozen parsley sprigs for instant chopped parsley.

# SALMON SAVOURY

## SERVES

### — 4 —

### INGREDIENTS

*2 onions, peeled and ringed*
*2 tablespoons sunflower oil*
*1 teaspoon curry powder*
*225 g (8 oz) brown rice, cooked*
*1 × 200 g (7 oz) can red salmon in water or brine, drained*
*3 eggs, hard-boiled and chopped*
*6 tablespoons evaporated milk*
*2 tablespoons fresh parsley, chopped*
**or** *2 teaspoons dried parsley*

Kedgeree originated in India but by the middle ages was being served as a breakfast dish in Britain. It is highly nutritious and requires only a mixed leaf salad to make it into a filling lunch or supper dish. This variation on kedgeree uses store-cupboard ingredients and is particularly suitable to rustle up quickly when unexpected guests arrive.

***Healthy Content:*** *Plenty of protein, vitamins A and D and the B complex as well as carbohydrate, calcium and some vitamin C in the parsley. Polyunsaturated fat in the salmon and some cholesterol in the egg yolks.*

Using a large saucepan, cook the onions in the heated oil until soft and golden. Stir in the curry powder, blend and cook for 30 seconds. Turn the heat off and set aside.

Stir cooked rice gently into onions. Flake in the salmon, discarding any skin or bones. Add the chopped eggs and evaporated milk.

Stir over a low heat for 2–3 minutes to heat through. Stir in the parsley, just before serving.

# PAN-FRIED
## TROUT WITH ORANGE

### S E R V E S
### —— 4 ——

This quick recipe must be one of the easiest ways to cook trout. Delicious pan-fried fish with an almost instant orange sauce – plain and simple yet high in flavour. Serve with potatoes and carrots boiled together in one pan with some frozen sweetcorn tossed into the pan towards the end of the cooking time.

*Healthy Content: Trout contains plenty of protein and is rich in polyunsaturated fat and vitamins A and D. The orange and parsley garnish adds vitamin C. Olive oil is high in healthy monounsaturates (good for the heart).*

▬▬▬▬

Season the flour with the dried parsley and the black pepper and use to coat the trout. Heat the oil in a large frying-pan, then add the fish and fry them until crisp and golden – allow about 5 minutes each side. Insert a vegetable knife into the thickest part of the fish to make sure it is cooked – it should go down easily to the bone. Transfer to a serving dish and keep warm.

Meanwhile, add the orange juice to the same pan, with any remaining flour. Bring to the boil, keep stirring and then simmer for 1–2 minutes, adding a little water if sauce becomes too thick.

Serve fish immediately, with the sauce and the garnish.

### INGREDIENTS

*4 rainbow trout, cleaned and gutted*
*4 tablespoons plain wholemeal flour*
*1 teaspoon dried parsley*
*Freshly ground black pepper*
*3 tablespoons olive oil*
*Juice of 2 oranges*

**TO SERVE**
*Fresh sprigs parsley*

# COD WITH HERBS AND AVOCADO SAUCE

### SERVES
### — 4 —

**FOR THE AVOCADO SAUCE**
1 ripe avocado
150 ml (5 fl oz) natural yoghurt
A little salt and freshly ground black pepper
Grated rind of
$^1/_2$ lime
1 tablespoon freshly chopped garden mint

**FOR THE FISH**
Juice of $^1/_2$ lime
Freshly ground black pepper
2 tablespoons fresh garden herbs, chopped
1 tablespoon olive oil
4 × 150 g (5 oz) cod steaks

Fresh, low fat cod steaks taste wonderful flavoured with herbs and lime juice, then grilled to perfection. The fish tastes particularly good when accompanied by the avocado sauce and a simple salad of watercress leaves and pink grapefruit segments. New potatoes, steamed in their skins, would make the meal complete.

***Healthy Content:*** *Plenty of protein. White fish is particularly easy to digest and it now seems that the monounsaturated fat in avocado is protective against heart disease. The yoghurt adds calcium.*

Make the sauce first so that it can be chilled whilst you prepare and cook the fish.

Peel and dice the avocado, retaining the stone. Put the avocado flesh into a food processor with all the remaining sauce ingredients. Process until smooth. If you don't have a processor, mash all the ingredients together with a fork. Turn into a serving dish and bury the stone in the sauce to prevent discoloration. Cover with clingfilm and chill.

To prepare the fish, arrange cod on grill rack, then mix together the lime juice, seasoning, herbs (parsley, thyme, mint, sage, basil etc) and olive oil. Spoon it evenly over the fish. Grill the fish for 4–5 minutes, carefully turning each steak over, once, half-way through cooking. Serve hot with the avocado sauce.

ORIENTAL CHICKEN COCKTAIL (*page 20*)

# MEXICAN COD

### S E R V E S
### —— 4 ——

Mexican food is fast becoming very popular in Britain. Many dishes are pretty high in fat as the natives of Mexico seem to serve full fat Cheddar cheese, avocado pear and fried corn pancakes called Tostada shells with just about every course, however rich.

These cod steaks are poached in an enchilada sauce and sprinkled with a little reduced fat Cheddar cheese on serving. While the cod is cooking, prepare a Mexican salad.

*Healthy Content: Plenty of calcium, protein with lots of fibre and vitamins in the salad.*

———

Gently warm the enchilada sauce in a large frying pan, then add the fish to the pan, in a single layer. Heat until just simmering and cook for 2 minutes. Carefully turn the fish over and poach for another 2 minutes or until fish is no longer opaque.

While the fish is cooking, make the Mexican salad. Place all the ingredients into a salad bowl and toss with a vinaigrette dressing.

To serve, lift fish onto serving dish, pour over the sauce, sprinkle with cheese and serve immediately with the salad.

### INGREDIENTS

1 × 265 g (approximately 9–10 oz) jar Discovery Foods enchilada sauce
4 thick cod cutlets
50 g (2 oz) reduced fat Cheddar cheese, grated

**FOR THE MEXICAN SALAD**

1 iceberg lettuce, shredded
1 red pepper, de-seeded and chopped
1 avocado pear, peeled and diced
1 small can red kidney beans, drained
4 tablespoons ready-made vinaigrette dressing

LIME AND CHERVIL HERRINGS (*page 36*)

# LIME AND CHERVIL HERRINGS

### S E R V E S
### —— 4 ——

**INGREDIENTS**

**FOR THE SAUCE**
*1 teaspoon ground ginger*
**or** *2.5 cm (1 inch) fresh*
   *ginger, grated*
*150 ml (5 fl oz) natural*
   *yoghurt*
*50 g (2 oz) pecan nuts,*
   *chopped*

**FOR THE FISH**
*4 herring fillets*
*Juice of ¹/₂ lime*
*1 tablespoon freshly*
   *chopped chervil*
*Freshly ground black*
   *pepper*

**TO GARNISH**
*¹/₂ lime, thinly sliced*
*1 sprig fresh chervil*

These herb-flavoured herrings are lovely with a cold yoghurt and nut sauce which counteracts the oiliness of the fish. Serve with pitta bread and salad. A lime garnish is well worth adding as it looks very pretty against the tawny coloured fish.

***Healthy Content:*** *Protein, calcium, polyunsaturated fat and vitamins A and D with some vitamin C are all present.*

Prepare the sauce first by combining the ginger, yoghurt and nuts. Cover and refrigerate.

Line your grill rack with tinfoil and arrange the herrings on it. Spoon over the lime juice, sprinkle evenly with chervil and season with a little black pepper.

Cook under a pre-heated grill turning once, for approximately 4–6 minutes, until fish is cooked. Garnish with lime and chervil and serve immediately with the sauce.

# HERBY SALMON PARCELS

**SERVES**

— 4 —

The sea, or salmon, trout is the only member of the salmon family that spends part of its life in the sea and part in the river.

Serve with warm pitta bread to complete this luxurious, tasty meal that's so quick and easy to make. Ideal for a dinner party to impress your friends.

**Healthy Content:** High in protein, polyunsaturated fats and vitamins A and D. The vegetables add fibre and vitamins.

---

Pre-heat the oven to gas mark 6, 400°F (200°C).

Arrange foil circles on baking sheet. Brush with a little of the oil to grease. Remove all bones from the fish and cut into strips. Divide between circles of foil.

Cut carrots and courgettes into matchsticks. Heat remaining oil and sauté the vegetables for 1 minute to soften slightly. Divide between foil. Add herbs and lemon juice. Season with black pepper.

Gather foil up loosely and close edges to form bag-like parcels. Bake for 10 minutes.

Allow guests to open up their parcels at the table.

**INGREDIENTS**

4 large circles of foil, about 25 cm (10 in) in diameter
2 tablespoons walnut oil
450 g (1 lb) salmon trout, skinned and filleted
5 small carrots, scrubbed clean
3 small courgettes
1 teaspoon dried mixed herbs
Juice of ½ lemon
Freshly ground black pepper

# SARDINE TOASTIES

### SERVES
### —— 4 ——

4 large thick slices lightly
   toasted wholemeal bread
Polyunsaturated margarine,
   for spreading
3 tomatoes, thinly sliced
1¹/₂ teaspoons dried basil
Freshly ground black
   pepper
150 g (5 oz) reduced fat
   Cheddar type cheese
2 × 120 g (4¹/₂ oz) cans
   sardines in water or
   brine, drained

Children and adults alike will love these simple toasties
and they are a convenient stand-by for a quick lunch
when friends drop in and decide to stay!

This snack looks good and can be served hot or cold. My
family loves them, for supper, in front of the television.

**Healthy Content:** *Plenty of carbohydrate, protein, calcium, fibre
and vitamins B and C. There is polyunsaturated fat in the sardines. Some saturated fat in the cheese.*

Lightly spread the toast with the margarine. Lay the tomato
slices all over each slice of toast, in a single layer. Sprinkle
evenly with the basil and season with the black pepper. Slice
the cheese, very thinly, using a cheese slicer, if available, and
divide between the toasties. Grill under a pre-heated
medium grill until lightly golden. Divide the sardines between the toasties and return to the grill to heat through.

# JAPANESE COD

**S E R V E S**

—— 4 ——

Stir-frying is fun, it's also quick and healthy. Make sure you have everything close to hand and all the vegetables prepared before you start to cook.

This colourful recipe is delicious with brown rice or noodles, but chunks of fresh wholemeal bread are fine if you've no time at all!

**Healthy Content:** *Fibre, protein, calcium, B vitamins and lots of vitamin C. The oil is high in polyunsaturated fat.*

---

Heat oil in a wok or large frying-pan. Add peppers, celery and mushrooms. Stir-fry over a medium heat for 4 minutes. Add cod and stir-fry for 3–4 minutes. Blend together tomato purée, soy sauce rind and the juice from the orange. Add these ingredients to the pan. Heat until bubbling.

Serve immediately.

### INGREDIENTS

*3 tablespoons corn oil*
*1 yellow pepper, de-seeded and cut into strips*
*1 red pepper, de-seeded and cut into strips*
*3 celery stalks, chopped*
*175 g (6 oz) small open mushrooms, sliced*
*450 g (1 lb) cod fillet, skinned and cubed*
*1 tablespoon tomato purée*
*1 tablespoon light soy sauce*
*Grated rind and juice of 1 orange*

# PRAWNS AND PEPPERS IN CIDER

### SERVES

— 4 —

### INGREDIENTS

*2 tablespoons sunflower oil*
*225 g (8 oz) frozen mixed peppers, sliced*
*1 red onion, peeled and sliced*
*1 clove garlic, peeled and crushed*
*175 g (6 oz) button mushrooms, sliced*
*1 tablespoon cornflour*
*300 ml (10 fl oz) dry cider*
*A little salt and freshly ground black pepper*
*450 g (1 lb) cooked peeled prawns*

Frozen prawns and peppers combined with onions and mushrooms in a cider sauce. Quick to cook and spectacular to serve to guests or family. Wholewheat noodles would be ideal with this colourful fishy dish.

**Healthy Content:** *Protein, calcium, vitamin C and fibre. The oil is high in polyunsaturated fat.*

Heat the oil in a wok or large frying-pan. Fry the peppers with the onion and garlic for about 3–4 minutes, until softened. Add the mushrooms and stir-fry for 2 minutes. Blend together the cornflour and cider and add to the pan. Bring to the boil, stirring, then simmer for 2 minutes. Season to taste. Add prawns, keep stirring and heat until the mixture starts bubbling.

Serve immediately.

# SUNFLOWER SALMON

### S E R V E S

—— 4 ——

The sunflower seeds give a pleasant crunchy texture to this dish. Serve with a mixed leaf salad and new potatoes. A quick dish to cook for entertaining or for a family celebration. Although this dish requires a little preparation in advance, as it is left to marinate, it cooks quickly and easily and looks stunning with the lime garnish and the red onion rings.

**Healthy Content:** *Salmon is rich in protein and vitamins A and D in the polyunsaturated fat. Sunflower seeds add a little polyunsaturated fat, calcium and fibre. Limes are rich in vitamin C.*

Put the walnut oil and vinegar into a mug. Whisk with a fork. Arrange the salmon steaks in a single layer in a shallow dish. Pour over marinade. Add onion rings and a seasoning of black pepper. Cover and refrigerate overnight or leave at room temperature for 20 minutes.

Remove onions and retain. Line the grill pan with foil and, using a fish slice, carefully lift salmon onto it. Cook under a pre-heated medium grill for about 4 minutes. Turn salmon steaks over. Top with reserved onion rings and sprinkle with sunflower seeds. Spoon over fish juices. Continue to cook for a further 4 minutes.

Serve immediately with the wedges of lime.

### INGREDIENTS

*2 tablespoons walnut oil*
*2 tablespoons red wine vinegar*
*4 × 175 g (6 oz) salmon steaks*
*1 red onion, peeled and sliced*
*Freshly ground black pepper*
*1 tablespoon sunflower seeds*

TO SERVE
*Wedges of lime*

**41**

# COD CURRY

### S E R V E S

### —— 4 ——

### INGREDIENTS

2 tablespoons sunflower oil

1 onion, peeled and
  chopped

1 clove garlic, peeled and
  crushed

1 tablespoon ground
  coriander

$^1/_2$ teaspoon turmeric

3 tablespoons coconut milk
  powder

150 ml (5 fl oz) warm
  water

1 × 400 g (14 oz) can
  chopped tomatoes

1 teaspoon dried parsley

750 g (1$^1/_2$ lb) cod fillet,
  skinned

1 tablespoon plain
  wholewheat flour

Cod is one of the cheapest white fish available and has a lovely delicate flavour. Serve with brown rice and salad or mange-tout. Fish curry is about the quickest of all curries to cook and it's filling too. Coconut milk powder is readily available, in boxes, in large supermarkets.

*Healthy Content: There is protein and polyunsaturated fat in the oil and a little saturated fat in the coconut milk. A beneficial amount of vitamin C.*

Heat the oil in a large saucepan. Add the onion, garlic, coriander and turmeric, and cook, stirring for 3 minutes. Blend the coconut powder with the warm water and add to the pan with the tomatoes and parsley. Bring to the boil and simmer for 2 minutes.

Meanwhile cut the cod into fairly large bite-size pieces and sprinkle with the flour.

Remove the pan from the heat and add the cod. Stir gently, bring to the boil, then cover and cook over a very gentle heat, stirring once or twice, for about 10 minutes, or until fish is cooked.

Serve immediately.

# TANGY HALIBUT

S E R V E S

—— 4 ——

Fish cooked with citrus fruit, a funny idea you may think, but the flavour of the fruit is so light and aromatic that it penetrates the delicate white flesh of the fish and the result is a flavour which is both summery and delicious. It looks pretty on the table too!

Serve the fish with a little of its juices poured over. Accompany it with new potatoes and blanched chopped leeks or fennel.

Cod or whiting may be used as an alternative.

**Healthy Content:** A low fat, high protein dish. Rich in vitamin C.

Pre-heat the oven to gas mark 4, 350°F (180°C).

Arrange the sliced fruit all over the base of a shallow dish. Top with the halibut, in a single layer. Arrange the bay leaves amongst the fish, pour over the wine and season with a little pepper.

Cover with foil and bake for about 20 minutes, until fish flakes easily and is no longer opaque. If you are using a microwave, cover the dish with clingfilm and microwave on 100 per cent full power for about 8–10 minutes. Serve immediately.

### INGREDIENTS

1 orange, sliced into rings
1 lemon, sliced into rings
1 lime, sliced into rings
4 halibut steaks, about
  175 g (6 oz) each
3 bay leaves
120 ml (4 fl oz) dry white
  wine, cider or apple juice
Freshly ground black
  pepper

# VEGETABLES AND
# INSTANT SALAD DISHES

These vegetable and salad recipes are all designed to be quick and simple to prepare, yet look stunning and taste delicious. I have also tried to make this section of recipes as varied as possible so that you have a salad or vegetable dish for just about every occasion.

Many of the recipes require very little cooking time – stir-frying and microwaving are two examples of especially speedy methods. The Spicy Dhal (see p. 54), which takes a little longer, can be cooked the day before, then served cold. It also re-heats successfully in the microwave.

Colourful, high fibre vegetables are full of vitamins and minerals; the fresher the vegetables the higher the vitamin content. Frozen vegetables are excellent too so I have included them as they are real time-savers.

Many vegetables have a high vitamin C content and shouldn't be left hanging around at any stage: during storage, preparation or before serving, as much of this fragile vitamin will be lost. You'll find, therefore, that the recipes cook vegetables 'tender crisp' and are designed to be served immediately.

Remember that salad (lettuce, cucumber etc) is largely comprised of water, with very few calories. To make a more substantial dish, nuts, pulses, dried fruits and other vegetables should all be combined with salad leaves to add fibre, protein and vitamins, texture and colour.

I've used few ingredients to produce speedy, yet pretty salads, often mixing fruit with the vegetables to this aim. You will find salad and vegetable dishes for all seasons amongst the recipes. Try Curried Coleslaw (see p. 55) – it's delicious in cheese sandwiches – but use a reduced fat cheese if possible.

The watercress, carrot and cheese in Dramatic Salad (see p. 50) is full of fibre, protein and flavour but still particularly quick and easy.

Fast vegetables and salads with plenty of colour mean health with a capital 'H' so step up on the amount you serve your family and cut down on other, less healthy foods.

# QUICK TIPS

• Don't peel vegetables unless absolutely necessary. Carrots, parsnips and potatoes are fine, scrubbed under a running tap.

• Cut vegetables into even sized pieces and cook in the minimum of boiling water: in a pan with a closely fitting lid or steam them if you prefer.

• Serve cold, left-over vegetables, tossed in a vinaigrette, as a salad.

• Add a tin of pulses to left-over vegetables to extend them.

• Add lightly cooked vegetables to a sauce and serve with rice or pasta for a quick and nutritious meal.

• Always use the cooking liquid from vegetables in a sauce or soup.

• Combine different colours and textures for interest.

• Don't add salt when you cook vegetables – they take longer to cook with it and taste better without it. Use herbs, lemon juice or garlic instead.

• Serve jacket potatoes with different fillings for quick meals. 4 potatoes will cook in 17–20 minutes in your microwave. Pierce each one before cooking and allow to stand for 5 minutes before serving. Serve with chopped ham and dates, tuna with spinach or walnuts and avocado.

• Remember, vegetables are rich sources of vitamins A and C, vitally important for our general good health.

# CHRISTMAS SALAD

**SERVES**

— 4 —

**INGREDIENTS**

*50 g (2 oz) walnuts, chopped*
*350 g (12 oz) red cabbage, finely shredded*
*3 large celery stalks, chopped*

**FOR THE DRESSING**
*5 tablespoons apple juice*
*Grated rind of ¹/₂ orange*
*3 tablespoons olive oil*
*1 small clove garlic, peeled and crushed*
*A little salt*
*Freshly ground black pepper*
*1 Cox's apple*

A high-fibre, very pretty salad that can be put together quickly with ingredients ready to hand. The red cabbage and celery look very Christmassy and the Cox's apple adds a good old English flavour. Serve with cold meats, but also good with hot pheasant, duck and chicken recipes. Once prepared this salad will keep for 2 days in the fridge.

***Healthy Content:*** *There is fibre with vitamins A and C and also some iron and calcium. Walnuts provide protein and polyunsaturates. Olive oil provides monounsaturates.*

Prepare the dressing first. Put the apple juice and the orange rind into a measuring jug. Add the olive oil and garlic. Season with the salt and pepper to taste. Whisk with a fork. Set aside.

Put the walnuts, cabbage and celery stalks into a salad bowl. Core and chop up the apple into rough pieces. Put them into the jug with the dressing and stir to coat so that the apple doesn't brown.

Pour the dressing (with the apple) into the salad bowl. Toss well to combine. Leave for 10–15 minutes to allow flavours to mingle and then serve.

# CRUNCHY
## VEGETABLE STIR-FRY

### SERVES
### — 4 —

Stir-frying is popular, quick and healthy. Very little oil is used and the vegetables are cooked so quickly that there is little loss of nutrients. The herbs and lemon juice in this recipe are healthy substitutes for salt.

Serve with boiled brown rice or noodles. Also delicious with the Cheesey Rice Tomatoes (see p. 24).

*Healthy Content: Plenty of fibre with vitamins A and C. Some carbohydrate in the sweetcorn. A little polyunsaturated fat in the walnut oil.*

---

Ensure all the vegetables are prepared and assembled, with the remaining ingredients, beside the cooker.

Heat the oil in a large frying-pan or wok. Add the vegetables with the garlic, oregano and 2 tablespoons of water. Stir continuously over a medium heat for 5–6 minutes until vegetables are just tender. Add lemon juice. Season with the pepper to taste.

Serve immediately.

**INGREDIENTS**

*2 tablespoons walnut oil*
*1 red pepper, de-seeded and sliced*
*100 g (4 oz) courgettes, topped, tailed and sliced at an angle*
*100 g (4 oz) carrots, scrubbed and cut into matchsticks*
*100 g (4 oz) baby sweetcorn, fresh or frozen, trimmed*
*100 g (4 oz) button mushrooms, sliced*
*2 cloves garlic, peeled and crushed*
*1/2 teaspoon dried oregano*
*Juice of 1/2 lemon*
*Freshly ground black pepper*

# SUNSHINE VEGETABLES

### SERVES

### — 4 —

*350 g (12 oz) young parsnips, scrubbed and thinly sliced*
*225 g (8 oz) young carrots, scrubbed and cut into matchsticks*
*6 tablespoons orange juice*
*1 teaspoon clear honey*
*2 teaspoons dried parsley*
*50 g (2 oz) walnuts, chopped*

This colourful vegetable dish is delicious served with stews and casseroles and it's quick and easy to make. The flavour of the root vegetables with the nuts is excellent, as are the two textures.

***Healthy Content:*** *There's carbohydrate, vitamin A and fibre in the vegetables. Some protein, vitamins and polyunsaturates in the walnuts.*

Put the parsnips and carrots into a medium-sized pan with the orange juice, honey and parsley. Cover with a tightly-fitting lid, bring to the boil and then simmer for 8–10 minutes. Alternatively, if you are using a microwave, put the vegetables, orange juice, honey and parsley into a casserole dish. Cover and microwave on 100 per cent full power for 7–8 minutes, stirring once, half-way through cooking.

Sprinkle with the chopped walnuts and serve.

# JACKET POTATOES WITH CHICKEN AND CHEESE

## SERVES

— 4 —

Jacket potatoes are a favourite amongst most people. If you have a microwave, this recipe is particularly quick. In this recipe potatoes are mixed with cold chicken, ham or turkey and celery and grilled until golden – the celery adds a delicious contrast in texture.

**Healthy Content:** *Plenty of carbohydrate, protein and vitamins as well as calcium. Potatoes are also a good source of vitamin C and fibre, particularly if you eat the skins too. Calcium is present in the milk and cheese. Low in fat.*

---

Pre-heat oven to gas mark 5, 375°F (190°C).

Pierce the potatoes in several places with a fork, then either place on a baking sheet and bake in a conventional oven for 1¹/₂ hours or, if you are using a microwave, arrange the potatoes in a circle and microwave on 100 per cent full power for 18 minutes, turn over once, half-way through cooking.

Remove potatoes from oven or microwave and allow to stand for 5 minutes. Carefully cut the potatoes in half, lengthways, allow to cool slightly and scoop out the potato flesh into a bowl, keeping the skins intact.

Mash the potato flesh with the milk, soft cheese and paprika. Stir in the celery, chicken, turkey or ham. Pile back into potato shells.

Pop under pre-heated grill until golden. Serve immediately. These potatoes re-heat well in the microwave if you prefer to prepare and grill them in advance. Allow approximately 2 minutes per ¹/₂ filled potato from the refrigerator.

## INGREDIENTS

*4 large jacket potatoes, each weighing about 225 g (8 oz)*

*6 tablespoons semi-skimmed milk*

*50 g (2 oz) low fat soft cheese with garlic and herbs*

*¹/₂ teaspoon paprika pepper*

*1 celery stalk, chopped finely*

*175 g (6 oz) skinned cooked chicken, turkey or smoked ham*

# SUMMER SALAD

### SERVES
#### —— 4 ——

This fruity salad is a simple combination of vegetables with strawberries, yet it looks stunning and is very colourful. Serve it on a large oval plate to make a change from a salad bowl. This recipe goes well with cold salmon and other meat and poultry dishes.

*Healthy Content: Plenty of fibre and vitamin C. Olive oil is rich in monounsaturates.*

---

**INGREDIENTS**

**FOR THE DRESSING**
4 tablespoons olive oil
Juice of 1 lime
1 tablespoon fresh mint,
    chopped
A little salt and freshly
    ground black pepper

**FOR THE SALAD**
1 lollo rosso lettuce
1 yellow pepper, de-seeded
    and cut into fine strips
225 g (8 oz) cherry
    tomatoes, halved
225 g (8 oz) strawberries,
    hulled and sliced

Put all the ingredients for the dressing into a mug and whisk with a fork.

Tear the lettuce leaves into bite-size pieces and put into a salad bowl. Add the strips of pepper, the tomatoes and strawberries. Pour over the dressing, toss to coat and serve immediately.

# DRAMATIC SALAD

### SERVES
#### —— 4 ——

Called 'dramatic' because of the vibrant colours, this quick salad is also highly nutritious. Serve with hard-boiled eggs or canned pilchards and crusty bread for a quick but complete meal.

*Healthy Content: Vitamins A and C, fibre, protein, calcium, polyunsaturated fat.*

---

**INGREDIENTS**

2 bunches watercress
3 medium carrots, scrubbed
    and grated coarsely
50 g (2 oz) reduced fat
    Cheddar cheese, grated
50 ml (2 fl oz) bottled
    French dressing, well
    shaken
Freshly ground black
    pepper

Arrange the watercress on an oval plate. Combine carrots and cheese then sprinkle onto the watercress.

Just before serving, pour over French dressing and sprinkle with the pepper.

# VEGETABLE CRUMBLE

### S E R V E S
### —— 4 ——

Tasty, high fibre vegetables make a delicious main meal dish when topped with a savoury crumble mixture. The parsley sauce keeps the vegetables moist during cooking and is quick and easy to prepare. You can make gravy, using the cooking liquid from the vegetables, if you prefer.

**Healthy Content:** *Carbohydrate and fibre with vitamins A and C. Calcium, protein and fat.*

———

Pre-heat the oven to gas mark 5, 375°F (190°C).

Put the prepared vegetables into a medium saucepan with 300 ml (10 fl oz) boiling water. Cover and simmer for about 10 minutes until vegetables are tender but still firm. Alternatively, if you have a microwave, put the vegetables into a dish with 3 tablespoons of water. Cover and microwave on 100 per cent full power for about 10–12 minutes, stirring once, half-way through.

Drain the vegetables and retain the liquid which should then be measured and made up to 300 ml (10 fl oz) with the semi-skimmed milk. Put the vegetables into baking dish, cover and keep warm.

Empty the sauce mix into a saucepan and stir in the milk mixture. Bring to the boil, stirring continuously. Simmer for 1–2 minutes, until boiled and thickened, then pour over the vegetables.

To prepare the topping, combine the flour, sesame seeds and oats. Fork in the oil and cheese. Spoon the crumble evenly over and bake towards top of oven for 20–25 minutes. Serve immediately.

**INGREDIENTS**

*350 g (12 oz) potatoes, diced*
*1 large carrot, scrubbed and sliced*
*225 g (8 oz) cauliflower florets*
*2 celery stalks, chopped*
*Semi-skimmed milk (see method)*
*1 × 25 g (1 oz) packet parsley sauce mix*

**FOR THE TOPPING**
*75 g (3 oz) wholemeal flour*
*2 tablespoons sesame seeds*
*50 g (2 oz) porridge oats*
*3 tablespoons sunflower oil*
*50 g (2 oz) Cheddar cheese, grated*

# SWEET-AND-SOUR FENNEL AND GRAPE SALAD

### S E R V E S
— 4 —

*1 head fennel*
*225 g (8 oz) small black*
  *seedless grapes*
*8 radishes, sliced*

**FOR THE DRESSING**
*4 tablespoons olive oil*
*2 tablespoons raspberry*
  *vinegar*
*A little salt and freshly*
  *ground black pepper*
*1 tablespoon snipped chives*

Fennel has a slightly aniseed flavour which complements the taste of grapes and radish. The raspberry flavour makes this recipe taste particularly fresh and fruity. A simple salad that looks spectacular and can be prepared two or three hours in advance.

***Healthy Content:*** *A good source of fibre with some vitamin C. Monounsaturated fat from the olive oil.*

Slice the fennel finely and put into a salad bowl. Add the grapes and radishes.

Put all the ingredients for the dressing into a mug, whisk to combine, and pour over the salad. Toss to coat.

Set aside for at least 15 minutes before serving to allow flavours to mingle.

# Saucy mediterranean vegetables

### SERVES
### — 4 —

A colourful array of filling vegetables cooked together in one pan for speed and convenience. An average serving of cauliflower will supply about half the daily requirement of vitamin C. Serve with chunks of bread or jacket potatoes.

**Healthy Content:** *Fibre, vitamin C and vitamin A with carbohydrate supplied by the accompanying bread or jacket potatoes.*

Heat the oil in a large saucepan and stir-fry the vegetables for 5 minutes. Mix together the stock, oregano and horseradish mustard with the red wine. Add to the rest of the ingredients, cover and simmer for 20 minutes.

Serve immediately.

### INGREDIENTS

1 tablespoon sunflower oil
1 aubergine, diced
1 red pepper, de-seeded and chopped
1 green pepper, de-seeded and chopped
350 g (12 oz) cauliflower florets
1 large carrot, cut into matchsticks
150 ml (5 fl oz) vegetable stock
1 teaspoon dried oregano
1 tablespoon horseradish mustard
2 tablespoons red wine or apple juice

# SPICY DHAL

**SERVES**

—— 4 ——

1 tablespoon corn oil
4 spring onions, chopped
1 clove garlic, peeled and crushed
1 large celery stalk, chopped
1 teaspoon ground coriander
225 g (8 oz) red lentils
600 ml (1 pint) chicken or vegetable stock

Lentils in the store-cupboard ensure a readily available cheap meal. The advantage of lentils compared to other dried pulses is that they do not need soaking before cooking.

Serve this filling, well-flavoured vegetable dish, hot or cold, with curries, meat and fish dishes.

*Healthy Content: Protein, carbohydrate, iron, calcium and B vitamins. Low in fat.*

Heat the oil in a large saucepan. Add the onions, garlic, celery and coriander. Fry gently for about 5 minutes, stirring frequently, until onions soften. Add the lentils and stir to coat with the oil. Add the stock, bring to the boil, then cover and simmer for 30 minutes.

Give the mixture a final stir and serve immediately. This recipe can also be served cold.

# CURRIED COLESLAW

S E R V E S

— 4 —

This healthy coleslaw is excellent with cold meat and cheese dishes. Use it in sandwiches too. It will keep for up to 2 days, covered, in the refrigerator.

*Healthy Content: The salad is high in fibre, vitamin C and vitamin A. The mayonnaise is made from sunflower oil, which is high in polyunsaturates.*

Shred the cabbage finely with a sharp knife and place in a large salad bowl. Add the carrot, onion and sultanas.

To make the dressing, put the egg, curry powder, salt and vinegar into a food processor. Blend for 10 seconds. With motor running, add the oil very slowly, through the lid – use the drip feed in the lid if you have one. After a short time the mayonnaise will thicken.

Add the prepared mayonnaise to salad bowl. Toss to mix well. Allow to stand for 10 minutes for flavours to mingle, then serve.

**INGREDIENTS**

*350 g (12 oz) white cabbage*
*225 g (8 oz) carrots, grated*
*1 onion, peeled and finely chopped*
*50 g (2 oz) sultanas*

FOR THE DRESSING

*1 egg*
*1 teaspoon curry powder*
*A little salt*
*2 teaspoons white wine vinegar*
*300 ml (10 fl oz) sunflower oil*

# PINK AND GREEN COLESLAW

### SERVES

### —— 4 ——

This high fibre, colourful salad looks very pretty on a buffet table or with barbecued food.

Coleslaw is quick to make as long as you have a sharp knife and a large chopping board – don't bother to use a food processor, it processes the cabbage too finely and is a bit of a bind to wash up afterwards!

***Healthy Content:*** *A high fibre salad rich in vitamin C. The fromage frais provides calcium for healthy bones and teeth. Dates add carbohydrate for energy. Low in fat.*

## INGREDIENTS

*150 g (5 oz) red cabbage*
*150 g (5 oz) white cabbage*
*8 radishes, sliced*
*75 g (3 oz) stoned dates, roughly chopped*

**FOR THE DRESSING**
*3 tablespoons tomato juice*
*120 ml (4 fl oz) fromage frais*
*2 teaspoons clear honey*
*2 teaspoons wholegrain mustard*
*A little salt and freshly ground black pepper*

Finely shred the red and white cabbage discarding any outside leaves and the tough core. Put into a large mixing bowl, add the radishes and toss lightly.

To make the dressing, combine the tomato juice, fromage frais, honey and mustard. Turn onto cabbage and season, lightly, to taste.

Finally add the dates, toss everything together until well-coated with dressing, turn into serving dish and chill until ready to serve.

# MEAT AND BACON

Simple to prepare, lean meat is healthy and can be cooked fast. Meat is the muscle tissue of an animal and consists of bundles of fibres, held together by connective tissue amongst which are fat cells. The fat provides energy and also gives meat its delicious flavour.

All meat, including gammon and ham, is an excellent source of high quality body-building protein as well as containing essential vitamins and minerals. The fat content of bacon is particularly reduced when bacon is grilled, especially when trimmed of visible fat before grilling.

Lean meat has a real place in a healthy diet and is lower in calories than you might think. Lean pork chops for example contain 73 calories per ounce, lean lamb chops about 80 calories whilst roast chicken breast has about 60 calories per ounce, so you can see that meat needn't be the weight-watcher's enemy.

Meat is rich in many of the B group of vitamins and helps to supply iron needed to make new blood cells and prevent anaemia.

I have used selected cuts that can be cooked fast, and healthy methods of cooking – grilling, dry-frying in non-stick pans and sealing, then draining off excess fat – to reduce the fat content of lean meat even further. During the war years, when meat was rationed, the nation's diet was forced to be fairly healthy with cooks quickly learning the art of extending the delicious flavour of a little meat with vegetables, pulses etc. We do the same today to create healthy recipes – notice the flavour of lamb in Lamb Provençal (see p. 59) and the Pork Burgers on p. 58 taste really meaty with a small amount of actual pork. The children will love them and the stir-fry recipes have plenty of vegetables to extend the meat.

# PORK BURGERS

### S E R V E S
### —— 4 ——

Lean pork is extended with breadcrumbs to m̶a̶k̶e̶ ̶t̶h̶e̶s̶e̶ tasty burgers. Serve with gravy, sweetcorn and mashed potatoes for a complete meal or in a wholemeal bap with relish and salad for a picnic.

**Healthy Content:** *Plenty of protein, B vitamins and minerals. The bread rolls provide fibre and carbohydrate. Some fat.*

Lightly oil the grill rack and pre-heat grill to a medium–hot temperature. Put all ingredients, including the bread, into a food processor and process until combined. Form into 4 even-sized balls and shape into burgers. Grill for about 7 minutes on each side, turning once.

Serve immediately.

**INGREDIENTS**

*Oil for greasing*
*275 g (10 oz) lean pork, minced*
*25 g (1 oz) wholemeal bread, without crusts, roughly broken*
*2 spring onions, chopped*
*1 tablespoon wine mustard*
*1 teaspoon dried parsley*
*1 egg, beaten*
*A little salt and freshly ground black pepper*

TO SERVE
*4 wholemeal baps*

# DEVILLED GAMMON

### S E R V E S
### —— 4 ——

'Devilled' simply means coating with a piquant paste, then grilling. Gammon has a wonderful flavour. These grilled steaks are excellent served with mashed potatoes, peas and a white wine sauce.

**Healthy Content:** *A good source of protein, iron and B vitamins, including some fat.*

Snip edges of gammon all round to prevent steaks curling during cooking. Lightly oil the grill rack and pre-heat grill on a medium temperature. Place the steaks on the rack and grill for about 4 minutes, turning over once.

Combine all the ingredients for the glaze, mix well, then brush liberally over the gammon. Continue to grill for approximately 3 minutes until cooked.

Serve immediately with a white wine sauce (see p. 97).

**INGREDIENTS**

*Oil for greasing*
*4 gammon steaks*

FOR THE GLAZE
*1 tablespoon olive oil*
*1 teaspoon lemon juice*
*1 teaspoon curry powder*
*1/2 teaspoon dried ginger*
*Freshly ground pepper*

# LAMB PROVENÇAL

### SERVES

### — 4 —

Lean minced lamb is readily available in most super-markets. This tasty meal is filling and nutritious. The cheese sauce (p. 92) is excellent served with this dish.

*Healthy Content: Plenty of protein, vitamins and fibre. Cheddar cheese alternative is made entirely from polyunsaturated sunflower oil. It tastes excellent, is great in cooking and a good source of calcium for healthy bones and teeth. Lamb contains vitamins and minerals, including iron, and some fat.*

Put the aubergines and the courgettes into a medium sauce-pan. Cover with boiling water and simmer gently for 5 minutes.

Meanwhile, put the mince into a dry frying-pan and stir over a medium heat until the meat browns. Drain the vegetables and add to frying-pan with the tomatoes and oregano. Season lightly. Continue to heat gently and keep stirring for 5 minutes. Turn into flameproof dish. Cover and keep warm.

To prepare the topping, put the cheese and bread into a food processor and process until lightly chopped. Stir in the sunflower seeds. Sprinkle the topping over the meat and vegetables to cover completely.

Pop under a pre-heated grill until golden. Serve immediately.

## INGREDIENTS

2 medium aubergines, diced
2 courgettes, sliced
350 g (12 oz) raw lean lamb, minced
4 tomatoes, skinned, de-seeded and chopped
$^1/_2$ teaspoon dried oregano
A little salt and freshly ground black pepper

**FOR THE TOPPING**

50 g (2 oz) Cheddar cheese alternative, cubed
3 slices from a wholemeal cut loaf, including crusts
2 tablespoons sunflower seeds

# SPEEDY LAMB
# WITH SPINACH

### S E R V E S
### —— 4 ——

*2 tablespoons corn oil*

*1 onion, peeled and chopped*

*1 clove garlic, peeled and crushed*

*450 g (1 lb) potatoes, diced*

*350 g (12 oz) raw lean lamb, minced*

*1 teaspoon dried mixed herbs*

*2 tablespoons tomato purée*

*250 ml (8 fl oz) stock*

*225 g (8 oz) frozen spinach leaf*

Minced lamb, potatoes and stock, simmered together in one pan, produce a delicious, well-flavoured main meal fast.

Serve with a mixed salad or the Spicy Dhal (see p. 54).

***Healthy Content:*** *Plenty of protein and carbohydrate, B vitamins and iron. Some fat. Spinach is rich in iron, calcium, vitamins A, C and fibre.*

Heat the oil in a large frying-pan or wok. Gently fry the onion and garlic for about 5 minutes until onion softens. Add the potatoes and lamb. Continue to fry, stirring frequently, until lamb starts to brown. Drain off any excess fat. Blend together the herbs, tomato purée and the stock. Add to the pan. Cover and simmer gently for 15 minutes and add the frozen spinach for the last 5 minutes of the cooking time.

Serve immediately.

# PORK WITH PARSLEY, PEPPERCORNS AND CIDER

S E R V E S

—— 4 ——

Beef steaks coated with peppercorns are frequently served in restaurants. Try my pork version which is just as delicious. The cider sauce has a lovely flavour and gives this recipe a particularly autumnal feel. This dish is wonderful with simple mashed potatoes (use semi-skimmed milk and low fat spread to mash them).

*Healthy Content: The pork provides protein, iron and B vit-amins and fat. The mashed potatoes add carbohydrate with some vitamin C.*

---

Put the peppercorns onto a chopping board and crush them with the back of a tablespoon. Then combine them and the parsley on a dinner plate. Brush both sides of each chop with oil, then coat with the peppercorns and parsley. Set aside for 10 minutes to allow the flavours to penetrate.

Heat a non-stick frying-pan, add the chops (turning them fairly quickly to seal both sides) then reduce the heat and continue to cook for about 8–10 minutes turning once or twice. Remove the chops, cover and keep warm. Add the cider to the pan, let it boil and reduce slightly.

Pour the cider sauce over the chops and serve immediately.

**INGREDIENTS**

3 teaspoons whole black peppercorns
3 tablespoons fresh parsley, chopped
4 boneless pork chops, trimmed of visible fat
2 tablespoons olive oil
150 ml (5 fl oz) dry cider or vegetable stock

# GAMMON,
## LEEKS AND PINEAPPLE

S E R V E S

—— 4 ——

2 tablespoons corn oil

225 g (8 oz) dwarf green
   beans, sliced

225 g (8 oz) leeks, sliced

5 cm (2 inch) piece root
   ginger, grated (optional)

350 g (12 oz) lean
   gammon, thinly sliced
   into strips

175 g (6 oz) frozen peas

1 × 225 g (8 oz) can
   pineapple pieces, in
   natural juice

2 tablespoons light soy
   sauce

Gammon cooks quickly in this easy stir-fry recipe. The canned pineapple and juice provide a quick sauce and add fibre and colour to the dish. Serve with noodles for a complete and attractive main course.

*Healthy Content: Protein, fat, iron and B vitamins from the gammon. Plenty of fibre and some vitamin C from the vegetables.*

Heat oil in a wok or large frying-pan. Stir-fry beans, leeks, ginger and gammon for 3 minutes. Add the peas with the pineapple and juice and finally the soy sauce. Bring to the boil, cover and simmer for 3 minutes.

Serve immediately.

# HAM AND EGG SMASH

**SERVES**

— 4 —

Serve this filling version of scrambled eggs on thickly sliced wholemeal toast at any time of the day.

**Healthy Content:** *Eggs are a valuable source of protein. They also contain iron (which helps prevent anaemia), vitamins A and D and B vitamins. Egg yolks do contain cholesterol so should take their place in a healthy diet 3 or 4 times a week.*

*Ham is a good source of protein with vitamins, minerals and some fat.*

Beat the eggs and milk together in a mixing bowl. Melt butter in a medium size non-stick saucepan and when it begins to sizzle, pour in the egg mixture. Add mushrooms and ham and season lightly. Cook over a gentle heat, stirring frequently until eggs are set (to your liking). This should take about 10 minutes.

Serve immediately on wholemeal toast.

**INGREDIENTS**

8 eggs
150 ml (5 fl oz) semi-
  skimmed milk
25 g (1 oz) butter
100 g (4 oz) button
  mushrooms, finely
  chopped in a food
  processor
100 g (4 oz) lean ham, cut
  into thin strips
A little salt and freshly
  ground black pepper

# RUMP STEAK
## WITH CRANBERRY SAUCE

### S E R V E S
### —— 4 ——

This mouthwatering dish is excellent for dinner parties and the tangy sauce provides a pleasant contrast to the rich meat. Serve with sweetcorn, green beans and jacket potatoes.

***Healthy Content:*** *Lean steak is an excellent source of protein. It is also a good source of iron and B vitamins. The steak contains some fat. There is vitamin C in the sauce.*

Trim any visible fat from the steaks. Heat a non-stick frying-pan and cook steaks over a medium heat for 4–5 minutes on each side or until cooked to your liking.

Meanwhile, prepare the sauce. Put the cranberry sauce and the orange juice into a saucepan. Blend the mustard and arrowroot with 1 tablespoon of water and stir into the sauce. Bring to the boil whilst stirring, then simmer for 1 minute, pass through a sieve and serve with the steaks.

**INGREDIENTS**

*4 × 175 g (6 oz) rump steaks*

**FOR THE SAUCE**

*3 tablespoons cranberry sauce*
*150 ml (5 fl oz) fresh orange juice*
*1 teaspoon dry mustard*
*1 teaspoon arrowroot*

# *B*EEF
## WITH WALNUTS

### S E R V E S
#### —— 4 ——

Use a packet of stir-fry sauce in this recipe for a true Chinese flavour, and for speed. You will find ready-made stir-fry sauces in your local supermarket.

High protein beef is extended with walnuts and cauliflower to provide a nutritious meal. Serve with rice or noodles.

*Healthy Content: Plenty of protein, iron and B vitamins in the steak with fibre in the nuts and vegetables. Peppers are rich in vitamin C. Some fat in the steak and walnuts.*

---

Parboil the cauliflower in boiling water for 3 minutes and drain. Heat the oil in a wok or large frying-pan. Stir-fry the steak, pepper and walnuts for about 3 minutes. Add the cauliflower and sauce and heat for 1–2 minutes whilst stirring.

Serve immediately.

### INGREDIENTS

*225 g (8 oz) cauliflower*
  *florets*
*2 tablespoons corn oil*
*350 g (12 oz) lean rump*
  *steak, cut into thin strips*
*1 red pepper, de-seeded and*
  *chopped*
*75 g (3 oz) walnut halves*
*1 standard size carton/jar*
  *hoisin sauce*

# LIVER STROGANOF

### S E R V E S
### —— 4 ——

2 tablespoons sunflower oil
1 onion, peeled and sliced
2 tablespoons plain
  wholemeal flour
A little salt and freshly
  ground black pepper
450 g (1 lb) lambs' liver,
  cut into strips
2 courgettes, cut into
  matchsticks
150 ml (5 fl oz) sour
  cream

TO SERVE
Mild paprika pepper

This recipe consists of strips of lambs' liver and match-sticks of courgette cooked quickly and served in a creamy sauce. Sour cream is produced by adding a special culture to single cream which gives it a sharp, yoghurt-like taste. You can easily make it yourself by adding 2 teaspoons of lemon juice to a 150-ml (5-fl oz) carton of single cream and leaving it to stand at warm room temperature for 15 minutes. The fat content of sour cream is approximately 18 per cent. Serve the stroganoff with jacket potatoes and peas.

**Healthy Content:** *Protein, iron, and fat from the lamb and some fibre from the courgettes. Fat and vitamin A from the cream.*

Heat the oil in a wok or large frying-pan, add the onion and stir-fry for 3 minutes. Season the flour with a little salt and freshly ground pepper and then toss the liver in it and add to the pan with the courgettes. Stir-fry for about 4 minutes or until the liver is cooked to your liking. Stir in the sour cream and heat through gently, stirring continuously.
  Serve immediately, sprinkled with the paprika pepper.

*Opposite:* CHRISTMAS SALAD (*page 46*)
*Overleaf:* SUNSHINE VEGETABLES (*page 48*)

# QUICK MAIN MEALS

To help you plan a complete main meal super-fast, I have provided attractive, quick and healthy complete courses in this section. Many of the dishes extend the staple protein foods with vegetables, rice or pasta to provide nutritionally balanced meals which are particularly low in fat.

For easy preparation and speed I have included a couple of quick and easy sauces and used bread mixed with sunflower seeds for an instant crispy savoury topping (see p. 76).

These recipes are particularly quick and easy because they contain few ingredients, which are quick to assemble and prepare. Have a sharp knife and chopping board ready.

Try Pork and Cashew Stir-Fry (see p. 77) which includes fresh grapefruit segments. Italian Pasta Bake (see p. 75) is a tasty filling dish with vegetarians in mind and Cheesey Ham Noodles (see p. 79) uses wholewheat noodles for extra fibre and the B group of vitamins. This recipe is served with a cheese sauce made from low fat evaporated milk instead of cream.

Extend these main meals into full menus by selecting a simple pud from the dessert section and choose a starter from the starter section if you're entertaining.

## QUICK TIPS

• Freeze stock in ice-cube trays to ensure a supply that will melt quickly.
• Keep some cooked brown rice in the refrigerator – it keeps for up to 5 days.
• Serve pasta with a quick to prepare packet sauce, a sauce made from a can of tomatoes, puréed in the processor or a sauce made up of cooked vegetables puréed with a little stock. Top with parmesan cheese and chopped parsley.
• Use the food processor for chopping raw vegetables fast as well as for puréeing cooked vegetables to make quick sauces.

*Opposite*: PERFECT FLORENTINE PIZZAS *(page 74)*
*Preceding page*: BEEF WITH WALNUTS *(page 65)*

• Use more peas, beans and lentils. They are cheap, filling, high in protein and low in fat.

• Buy canned vegetables, including baked beans with no added sugar, and make good use of them.

• Serve wholemeal bread with your meal if you haven't time to cook potatoes or rice.

• Use as little oil or fat as possible in cooking and choose one that is low in saturates such as sunflower, soya, corn or olive oil.

## FISHY DISH

S E R V E S

—— 4 ——

A quick fish dish using frozen cod steaks and tomatoes. Serve this high protein meal with potatoes and a leaf salad. An ideal supper dish for informal entertaining.

*Healthy Content: High in protein, vitamin C. Some fibre. Potatoes add carbohydrate, fibre and vitamin C.*

Place the cod steaks in a large frying-pan. Add the water, bay leaves and a seasoning of black pepper. Bring to the boil. Cover and simmer for about 7 minutes or until fish is no longer opaque. If you are using a microwave the cod steaks will take about 12–15 minutes to defrost on the defrost setting.

Lift the fish steaks onto a serving plate. Cover and keep warm. Blend the puréed tomatoes with the tomato purée and add to the fish juices. Stir and heat gently, until simmering. Serve 2 cod steaks per person with the tomato sauce.

**INGREDIENTS**

8 × 92 g (3¹/₂ oz) frozen
  cod steaks, defrosted
4 tablespoons water
2 bay leaves
Freshly ground black
  pepper
1 × 400 g (14 oz) can
  chopped tomatoes, with
  herbs, puréed
3 tablespoons tomato purée
**TO SERVE**
Fresh parsley, chopped, or
  grated Parmesan cheese

## PEANUT RICE FIESTA

S E R V E S

—— 4 ——

This super-fast meal uses cooked rice and frozen mixed vegetables. This is a filling meal that is ideal for vegetarians – it's also well-flavoured. Serve with crusty bread.

*Healthy Content: High in carbohydrate and fibre, vitamins, some polyunsaturated fat. Peanuts supply some protein.*

Roast the peanuts in the microwave for 4–5 minutes.

Put the mixed vegetables into a large saucepan with the stock. Cover, bring to the boil and simmer for 3 minutes. Add the cooked rice, peanuts, bean sprouts, a seasoning of black pepper and the sukiyaki sauce. Heat through thoroughly, stirring occasionally. Serve immediately.

**INGREDIENTS**

75 g (3 oz) peanuts
1 × 350 g (12 oz) packet
  frozen mixed vegetables
120 ml (4 fl oz) chicken
  stock
450 g (1 lb) cooked, chilled
  brown rice
1 × 410 g (14¹/₂ oz) can
  bean sprouts, drained.
Freshly ground black
  pepper and 3 tablespoons
  sukiyaki sauce

# PERFECT FLORENTINE PIZZAS

S E R V E S

—— 4 ——

275 g (10 oz) frozen
    spinach leaf
2 cloves garlic, peeled and
    crushed
4 tablespoons tomato purée
2 teaspoons dried mixed
    herbs
2 spring onions, chopped
2 freshly baked batons
150 g (5 oz) Mozzarella
    cheese, grated
2 × 120 g (4¹/₂ oz) cans
    sardines in water or
    brine, drained (or 100 g
    (4 oz) lean ham cut into
    thin strips)

This home-made version of French bread pizza is quick and easy to prepare and tastes authentic. Serve straight from the oven with a crisp mixed salad or slice the pizzas and serve with drinks.

Batons are half the size of French bread sticks and available from the bakery counter of your supermarket.

**Healthy Content:** High in carbohydrate, protein, calcium, fibre, vitamin C, iron and B vitamins.

Pre-heat the oven to gas mark 8, 450°F (230°C).

Put the frozen spinach into a medium-sized saucepan with 1 tablespoon of water. Cover and heat for 3–4 minutes until completely thawed. Stir in the garlic, tomato purée, 1 teaspoon of the mixed herbs and the onions.

Cut the batons in half lengthways and arrange on a baking sheet. Divide spinach mixture between the bread, spreading it over evenly. Top with the cheese. Cut sardines in half lengthways and space out over the cheese. Sprinkle over with remaining teaspoon of mixed herbs and bake for about 10–12 minutes until the cheese melts. Serve immediately.

# ITALIAN PASTA BAKE

S E R V E S

— 4 —

Mozzarella cheese is low in calories and highly versatile. Try it in this quick pasta recipe which is delicious served hot with French bread and salad. Any left-overs can be served as a pasta salad the next day.

***Healthy Content:*** *High in carbohydrate with some protein, B vitamins, fat and calcium. Vitamin C in the cauliflower and tomatoes.*

---

Pre-heat the oven to gas mark 6, 400°F (200°C).

Cook the pasta in a large pan of boiling water, with the oil, until tender. For the cooking time refer to the directions on the packet (should be about 8–10 minutes). Add the cauliflower after the first 5 minutes. Drain well and return to the pan. Add all the remaining ingredients except the Edam. Mix gently and turn into an ovenproof dish. Top with the grated Edam.

Bake for 10–15 minutes, until cheese has melted and ingredients are piping hot. Serve immediately.

### INGREDIENTS

*225 g (8 oz) pasta shapes*
*2 teaspoons olive oil*
*225 g (8 oz) cauliflower florets*
*1 × 400 g (14 oz) can chopped tomatoes with herbs*
*100 g (4 oz) Mozzarella cheese, cubed*
*1 clove garlic, peeled and crushed*
*50 g (2 oz) Edam cheese, grated*

# BEAN FEAST

### S E R V E S

—— 4 ——

### INGREDIENTS

1 tablespoon olive oil

1 onion, peeled and
  chopped

100 g (4 oz) frozen
  sweetcorn kernels with
  peppers

1 × 400 g (14 oz) can red
  kidney beans

1 × 400 g (14 oz) can
  borlotti beans

1 × 400 g (14 oz) can
  chopped tomatoes

1 teaspoon hot chilli
  powder

1 teaspoon dried thyme

### FOR THE TOPPING

3 slices from a wholemeal
  cut loaf, including crusts

50 g (2 oz) Blue Cheshire
  or mature Cheddar
  cheese

25 g (1 oz) sunflower seeds

N eeding a super-fast lunch when a vegetarian friend
called in unexpectedly, I developed this recipe which
proved extremely popular with all of us.

This recipe contains a nice contrast of textures with the
crispy topping. Serve with coleslaw and chunks of wholemeal bread for a complete meal.

***Healthy Content:*** *Rich in protein, fibre and carbohydrate. Lots
of B vitamins and also iron in the pulses. Low fat.*

Heat the oil in a large saucepan, then fry the onion for about
5 minutes until tender. Add the sweetcorn and stir-fry for 3
minutes. Drain and rinse the beans, then add to the pan with
the tomatoes, chilli powder and thyme. Heat slowly, stirring, until everything is thoroughly hot. Then turn into
baking dish.

Meanwhile, prepare the topping. Put the bread (roughly
torn into pieces) and the cheese (cut into 4 or 5 pieces) into
a food processor. Process until mixture resembles
breadcrumbs.

Add sunflower seeds to topping and sprinkle evenly over
bean mixture. Brown under pre-heated grill. Serve
immediately.

# PORK AND CASHEW STIR-FRY

### S E R V E S
### —— 4 ——

Fruit, nuts and pork combine well in this interesting healthy dish. The cashew nuts add texture. Serve with rice or noodles.

*Healthy Content: Protein, fibre, vitamins B and C. Iron (carbohydrate in the rice or noodles). Some fat.*

Peel one grapefruit, removing all the pith. Cut into segments, discarding skin and membrane. Squeeze the juice from the other and reserve.

Heat the oil in a wok or large frying-pan. Add the cashew nuts and stir-fry until lightly browned. Remove with a draining spoon and blot on kitchen paper.

Add the pork and chillies to the pan and again stir-fry until lightly browned. Add the broccoli and pepper and continue to cook for 4 minutes, until just tender. Stir the grapefruit juice and honey into the pan. Bring to the boil. Add the grapefruit segments and cashew nuts and stir until heated through.

Serve immediately.

## INGREDIENTS

2 pink grapefruit

2 tablespoons corn oil

50 g (2 oz) cashew nuts

350 g (12 oz) pork fillet, thinly sliced

1 teaspoon dried chillies, crushed

225 g (8 oz) broccoli florets

1 red pepper, de-seeded and sliced

1–2 teaspoons clear honey

# GLAZED LAMB
# WITH SOY MUSHROOMS

### SERVES
### —— 4 ——

*4 British lamb steaks or*
*chump chops*
*4 teaspoons wholegrain*
*mustard*
*2 teaspoons clear honey*

**FOR THE SOY**
**MUSHROOMS**

*350 g (12 oz) button*
*mushrooms, sliced*
*2 tablespoons olive oil*
*1 tablespoon soy sauce*

S heep live most of their lives out of doors and are reared on natural food sources. Lean lamb rightfully deserves a true place in a healthy diet. Serve with new potatoes, boiled in their skins.

***Healthy Content:*** *Lamb is high in protein, iron, and B vitamins, as well as supplying some fat. Olive oil is rich in monounsaturated fat.*

Trim any visible fat from the chops and discard.

Pre-heat the grill to medium-hot, then cook the chops on one side for about 7 minutes. Turn the steaks over and continue to grill for 3–4 minutes. Mix together mustard and honey and spread on the lamb. Grill for a further 3–4 minutes, until cooked.

Meanwhile, heat the oil in a large frying-pan. Add the mushrooms with the soy sauce and cook for about 5–7 minutes, stirring frequently, until mushrooms are crisp. Pour over lamb steaks and serve immediately.

# CHEESEY
# HAM NOODLES

### S E R V E S
### —— 4 ——

Wholewheat noodles have a subtle nutty taste. They are simplicity itself to cook and the creamy sauce used in this recipe tastes as though it was made from full fat cream, yet it uses low fat evaporated milk and is super-quick to use. Vary the ham with chicken or sautéd mushrooms for a change.

**Healthy Content:** *High in carbohydrate and fibre. There is also protein, calcium and B vitamins. Low in fat. Calcium in the cheese and milk.*

---

Add the noodles to a large pan of boiling water. Remove the pan from the heat, cover and leave to stand for 5 minutes.

Blend the cornflour with 1 tablespoon of water. Then place in a separate medium-sized saucepan and add the evaporated milk, cheese and garlic. Heat and stir gently until the mixture boils and thickens. Simmer for 1–2 minutes. Add the ham. Season with pepper to taste.

Stir and drain the pasta and put onto warm serving plates. Top with the sauce and serve immediately.

### INGREDIENTS

*225 g (8 oz) wholewheat pasta noodles*
*2 teaspoons cornflour*
*1 × 410 g (15 oz) can low fat evaporated milk*
*75 g (3 oz) reduced fat mature Cheddar cheese*
*1 clove garlic, peeled and crushed*
*100 g (4 oz) smoked lean ham, cut into strips*
*Freshly ground black pepper*

# PERFECT
## PIZZA PIE

### S E R V E S
### — 4 —

A deliciously light pizza, well-flavoured with herbs. Serve straight from the oven with a bowl of mixed salad or halved cherry tomatoes tossed with some watercress and a ready-made French dressing.

*Healthy Content: High in carbohydrate. The topping supplies fibre, vitamins, protein, calcium and some fat from the cheese.*

Pre-heat the oven to gas mark 7, 425°F (220°C).

Heat 1 tablespoon olive oil in a frying pan, then fry the courgettes, onion, garlic and mushrooms for about 5 minutes, or until softened. Set aside.

Prepare the base. Put the flour and mixed herbs into a mixing bowl. Add corn oil and milk and mix well to form a dough. Knead lightly, then either roll out or push out with your hands to fit a lightly oiled Swiss roll tin, about 33 × 23 cm (13 × 9 in).

Spread the mushroom mixture over the dough, cover with the tomatoes, sprinkle with the oregano, season with a little salt and freshly ground black pepper and then lay the cheese slices on top. Sprinkle the remaining olive oil all over pizza. Bake for 10 minutes, then reduce heat to gas mark 6, 400°F (200°C) and bake for a further 10–15 minutes, until melted and golden. Serve immediately.

### INGREDIENTS

2 tablespoons olive oil

2 courgettes, sliced

175 g (6 oz) onion, peeled and chopped

1 clove garlic, peeled and crushed

100 g (4 oz) mushrooms, sliced

350 g (12 oz) tomatoes, thinly sliced

1 teaspoon dried oregano

A little salt and freshly ground black pepper

175 g (6 oz) Swiss Emmental cheese, thinly sliced

**FOR THE SCONE BASE**

225 g (8 oz) super-fine wholemeal self-raising flour

1 teaspoon dried mixed herbs

2 tablespoons corn oil

About 150 ml (5 fl oz) semi-skimmed milk

# PORK WITH MUSTARD SAUCE AND TOMATOES

### S E R V E S
### —— 4 ——

Fat-trimmed, ready-stuffed, boneless chump chops bought from the supermarket are quick to grill with some cheesey topped tomatoes alongside them. The mustard sauce is made by the foolproof one-stage method of putting everything in one pan together and heating gently until the mixture boils and thickens. I can assure you that this sauce never goes lumpy.

Serve this well balanced main meal with salad and pitta bread for speed and convenience.

*Healthy Content: Protein, iron, B vitamins, calcium, fat.*

―――――

Cook chops under a pre-heated medium grill for about 10 minutes on each side, or until well cooked. Ten minutes before serving, halve the tomatoes horizontally and add to grill pan. Combine 15g (¹/₂ oz) of the cheese with the oregano and divide between each tomato.

Meanwhile, make the sauce. Put all the ingredients, except the mustard, into a saucepan and heat gently, stirring constantly until boiling. Simmer for 2–3 minutes. Remove from the heat. Stir mustard and remaining cheese into sauce until cheese melts.

Serve immediately with the chops and tomatoes.

## INGREDIENTS

4 ready-stuffed, boneless chump pork chops
2 large tomatoes
40 g (1¹/₂ oz) Cheddar cheese, finely grated
1 teaspoon dried oregano

**FOR THE MUSTARD SAUCE**
300 ml (¹/₂ pint) semi-skimmed milk
2 tablespoons plain wholemeal flour
25 g (1 oz) polyunsaturated margarine
Freshly ground black pepper
1 tablespoon wholegrain mustard

# CHICKEN PILAFF

P ilaff is an Eastern dish of rice cooked with various spices and fruits. Fried onion rings, toasted almonds or cashew nuts are often added to this dish as a garnish.

For speed and convenience the whole meal is cooked in one saucepan.

***Healthy Content:*** *High in carbohydrate, protein, fibre and B vitamins. Low fat.*

## INGREDIENTS

*2 tablespoons corn oil*
*2 cloves garlic, peeled and chopped*
*275 g (10 oz) easy-cook wholegrain rice*
*175 g (6 oz) button mushrooms, sliced*
*3 tomatoes, skinned, de-seeded and chopped*
*50 g (2 oz) stoned raisins*
*900 ml (1¹/₂ pints) chicken or vegetable stock*
*250 g (9 oz) cooked chicken meat or quorn, diced*

**TO GARNISH**
*50 g (2 oz) flaked almonds, toasted*
or *1 tablespoon fresh parsley, chopped*

Heat the oil in a large saucepan. Add the garlic, rice, mushrooms and tomatoes. Stir well over a gentle heat for 2 minutes. Add the raisins and the stock. Bring to the boil, cover and simmer for 15 minutes, or until the water has been more or less absorbed and the rice is tender. Remove from the heat, keep covered and stand for 5 minutes.

Stir in the chicken meat or quorn and re-heat over a low heat for 3–4 minutes.

Serve, sprinkled with the almonds or chopped parsley.

## RAPID RICE & PASTA MEALS

## RICE

There are three main sizes of rice grain – long, medium and short. The long grains separate in cooking and are ideal for savoury rice dishes. Short grain is used mainly for sweet rice dishes such as rice pudding.

*Brown rice* consists of the whole natural grain with the inedible outer husk removed. In *white rice*, the hulls, germ and most of the bran layers have been removed resulting in a more bland product which has very little flavour once cooked. However, it easily takes on the flavour of other foods, has a good texture and is still a valuable energy-giving food.

*Frozen cooked rice* is an ideal convenience product which cooks quickly. It is available from major supermarkets and often comes mixed with vegetables. Follow directions on packet for cooking instructions.

*Wild rice* is, confusingly, not actually rice at all, but seeds of wild grains used for savoury dishes. It is expensive, but a little goes a long way and, when mixed with other rice, the result is both dramatic and exotic – it's excellent served with Japanese food or pheasant dishes.

### PERFECT RICE

There are many methods available for cooking rice but I find this the best as it is always successful and produces perfect, free-flowing grains. Make sure you measure both the rice and the water in the same liquid measuring jug.

Serves 4
*300 ml (10 fl oz) long-grain rice*
*600 ml (1 pint) cold water*

Wash the rice in a sieve and put into a 1.75-litre (3-pint) pan. Add the water, cover with a lid and bring to the boil. Keep covered and simmer gently. Allow 12–15 minutes for white rice and 30–35 minutes for brown rice. Remove from heat and test rice, which should be tender but firm and just about all the water should have been absorbed by the rice. Leave to stand for 2–3 minutes. Fluff up and serve immediately.

### MICROWAVE RICE

Whilst white rice cooks in the same time it would take in a conventional cooker, brown rice is much quicker. Both white and brown rice give perfect results cooked the microwave way and never become sticky.

Serves 4
*300 ml (10 fl oz) long-grain rice, white or brown*
*650 ml (22 fl oz) boiling water*
*1 teaspoon corn oil*

Put the rice into a covered bowl with the water and oil. For white rice, micro-wave on high for 10 minutes and leave to stand, still covered, for 10 minutes. For brown rice, microwave on high for 22 minutes and stand for 12 minutes.

### STORING COOKED RICE

Cooked rice, once cooled and covered, will keep in the refrigerator for 4–5 days without any deterioration. To re-heat bring it to the boil in a large pan of cold water (300 ml or 10 fl oz). Simmer gently for about 5 minutes, then drain and serve.

This cooked rice is also excellent in all super-quick stir-fry recipes and in rice salads.

# PASTA

Whilst spaghetti remains the traditional pasta favourite, recent years have seen a growing inclination towards the many varieties of pasta now on offer.

The best pasta is made from durum wheat semolina. This is a hard wheat which doesn't break down during cooking. In egg pasta the semolina has been enhanced with egg and is a richer, more yellow colour. Green pasta has had spinach added to it, while red pasta is coloured with tomatoes. Some specialist delicatessens sell more obscure pasta – I recently tried one made with beetroot!

Pasta is low in fat, an excellent source of carbohydrate and a reasonable source of protein. It is often wrongly thought to be high in calories, whereas in fact it is the sauce accompaniments which are often the unhealthy element of the dish – a 75 g (3 oz) serving of pasta, which is far more than I can ever eat, yields approximately 285 calories. It's filling and its slow conversion into energy when digesting is beneficial not only to marathon runners, but also to everyone who leads an active life!

Pasta comes in so many shapes and sizes it can be difficult to choose which type to serve with which sauce. As a simple guide, the longer, thinner varieties, such as spaghetti and fettuccine, are suitable for the thinner sauces – e.g. Spaghetti Carbonara and Spaghetti Napoletana. Use the pretty shapes such as shells and spirals for thicker sauces which adhere to the folds and crevices of the pasta shapes. Make use, too, of the tiny varieties which can be added to soups.

**PERFECT PASTA**

All pasta can be cooked using the same method. Use this foolproof method for perfect pasta which is guaranteed not to stick.

Serves 4
*2.25 litres (4 pints) water*
*2 teaspoons olive oil*
*350 g (12 oz) pasta (try to use a good quality brand)*

Fill a large, heavy-based pan with the water and olive oil, cover and bring to the boil.

Empty the pasta into the boiling water. If you are using spaghetti, grasp it in a bundle and gently push it into the boiling water as it softens until it is completely immersed. For other types of pasta, simply add to boiling water.

Stir the pasta several times during cooking with a wooden spoon to prevent it sticking. Return water to the boil, then simmer, uncovered, for 8–10 minutes checking it at regular intervals until it becomes *al dente* (slightly firm to the bite). Good pasta should be tender but still firm.

Before serving, drain the pasta in a colander but remember that a little cooking water left on the pasta will help the sauce to stick to it.

## QUICK TIPS

• Pasta for use in a salad should be rinsed with cold water or drained, then immediately tossed in an olive oil dressing and allowed to cool.
• Adding a chicken or vegetable stock cube to the water when you cook pasta gives a delicious flavour.
• High fibre wholewheat pasta takes a little longer to cook (allow 10–15 minutes), whilst quick-cooking pasta only takes 7–8 minutes and soup pasta, added to simmering home-made soup, takes only 4 minutes.
• Noodles are very thin strands of pasta made from either wholegrain or white flour. They are particularly quick to cook (3–4 minutes in boiling water).

# VEGETARIAN RICE

### SERVES
— 4 —

This filling and colourful rice dish is popular with vegetarians. A well-flavoured, high fibre dish that is complete in itself.

*Healthy Content: Fibre, B vitamins, carbohydrate in the rice and beans. There is iron and protein in the beans. Vitamin C in the vegetables. Walnut oil is rich in polyunsaturates.*

## INGREDIENTS

4 tablespoons walnut oil

1 onion, peeled and chopped

1 red pepper, de-seeded and chopped

2 celery stalks, chopped

175 g (6 oz) brown rice

2 cloves garlic, peeled and crushed

600 ml (1 pint) hot vegetable stock or water

175 g (6 oz) button mushrooms, sliced

1 × 430 g (15 oz) can red kidney beans, drained

2 teaspoons dried parsley

Heat 2 tablespoons of the oil in a large saucepan. Add the onion, red pepper and celery and fry until softened. This should take about 5 minutes. Add the rice and garlic, and stir for 1 minute. Add the stock or water and bring to the boil. Cover and simmer gently for 30 minutes until most of the water has been absorbed and the rice is tender. Add the mushrooms, beans and parsley. Keep stirring and heat through thoroughly before serving.

# WHOLEWHEAT NOODLES WITH CREAM CHEESE SAUCE

### SERVES
— 4 —

A quick pasta dish which tastes rich and delicious. Serve with French bread and a mixed salad.

*Healthy Content:* Carbohydrate, B vitamins and fibre. Protein and calcium in the fromage frais.

---

Prepare the sauce first. Put the celery into a small bowl with 1 tablespoon water. Cover and microwave on 100 per cent full power for 3 minutes. Set aside. Put the cream cheese into a medium-sized saucepan and season with the black pepper. Blend in the tomato purée and the fromage frais. Heat gently and stir until very hot but not boiling. Stir the celery with any residual liquid into the sauce.

Add the noodles to a large pan of boiling water, return to the boil and cover. Remove from the heat and leave to stand for 5 minutes. Drain the noodles, arrange on serving dish and top with the celery sauce.

Serve sprinkled with the Parmesan.

## INGREDIENTS

**FOR THE SAUCE**
3 celery stalks, finely chopped
1 × 150 g (5 oz) carton low fat soft cheese with garlic and herbs
Freshly ground black pepper
1 tablespoon tomato purée
300 ml (10 fl oz) fromage frais
1 × 250 g (9 oz) packet wholewheat noodles

**TO SERVE**
Grated Parmesan cheese

# HEALTHY
## SPAGHETTI BOLOGNE

### S E R V E S
#### — 4 —

**FOR THE BOLOGNESE SAUCE**

*1 tablespoon corn oil*

*2 onions, peeled and chopped*

*1 rasher back bacon, rinded and chopped*

*225 g (8 oz) lean minced beef*

*1 teaspoon dried oregano*

*100 g (4 oz) red lentils, washed*

*1 × 400 g (14 oz) can chopped tomatoes*

*150 ml (5 fl oz) beef stock*

*2 tablespoons tomato purée*

*1 clove garlic, peeled and crushed*

*A little salt and freshly ground black pepper*

*275 g (10 oz) long spaghetti*

*2 teaspoons olive oil*

**TO SERVE**

*Grated Parmesan cheese*

In this recipe, lean minced beef is extended with lentils and tomatoes so that 225 g (8 oz) will feed four people. During the war years, when meat was so scarce, people learned to extend meat with other foods and consequently adopted a far healthier diet than we do today.

Buy meat which is actually labelled 'lean' for this recipe. A filling, nutritious meal that needs no more than a leaf salad to accompany it.

***Healthy Content:*** *High in carbohydrate, protein, fibre, iron and B vitamins. Some fat.*

To make the sauce, heat the oil in a large pan, then fry the onions and bacon for about 5 minutes until onions soften. Add the beef and fry until the meat browns – drain off any excess fat. Add the oregano, lentils, tomatoes, stock, tomato purée and garlic. Stir well and season. Bring to the boil, cover and simmer gently for 30 minutes.

Cook the spaghetti in a large pan of boiling water and the olive oil until just tender. This should take approximately 8–10 minutes but look at directions on the packet too. Drain and turn onto a serving dish. Top with the bolognese sauce, sprinkle with the Parmesan cheese and serve immediately.

# TORTELLINI
## SOUP

### S E R V E S
#### —— 4 ——

This filling soup is a meal in itself when served with chunks of fresh granary bread. Tortellini is shaped pasta filled with chicken or cheese. This recipe uses Tortellini Verdi, a spinach-flavoured pasta with a cheese filling.

For speed and convenience the whole meal is cooked in one large pan. A delicious and original lunch, or supper dish with an Italian twist.

**Healthy Content:** *High in carbohydrate. Also protein, fibre and a little vitamin C.*

————

Using a large saucepan, heat the oil and fry the onion over a gentle heat for about 5 minutes or until the onion softens. Add the stock, tomatoes, pasta and the parsley. Bring to the boil, stirring occasionally.

Simmer for 15 minutes, then add the lemon juice and season with the black pepper. Remove from heat. Blend the cornflour to a smooth paste with a little water and stir into the soup. Return to the boil, keep stirring, simmer for 1–2 minutes, then serve immediately.

### INGREDIENTS

1 tablespoon corn oil
1 large onion, peeled and
   roughly chopped
1.5 litre (2¹/₂ pints) well-
   flavoured chicken stock
2 tomatoes, peeled, de-
   seeded and chopped
100 g (4 oz) Tortellini
   Verdi (with cheese
   filling)
3 teaspoons dried parsley
2 teaspoons lemon juice
Freshly ground black
   pepper
2 tablespoons cornflour

# SPICED QUORN KEDGEREE

### S E R V E S
### —— 4 ——

1 tablespoon corn oil
1 onion, peeled and
  chopped
1 teaspoon curry powder
225 g (8 oz) white rice
Juice ½ lemon
750 ml (1¼ pints) hot
  chicken stock
250 g (9 oz) quorn,
  roughly chopped
1 hard-boiled egg, chopped
2 tablespoons fresh parsley,
  chopped
2 tablespoons sour cream or
  fromage frais

Quorn is a nutritious new food which makes a versatile alternative to meat or fish. Vegetable in origin, quorn is derived from a distant relative of the mushroom. People often mistake quorn for chicken when it is used in this recipe – it certainly fills you up as quickly as chicken does. Quorn is available on the chill counter in your local supermarket.

A delicious and healthy kedgeree which makes an ideal lunch or supper dish.

***Healthy Content:*** *Plenty of fibre, protein and carbohydrate. Vitamin C in the fresh parsley. Low fat.*

Using a large saucepan heat the oil and fry the onion for about 5 minutes or until the onion softens. Add the curry powder and the rice. Stir-fry for 1 minute. Add the lemon juice and the stock. Bring to the boil, cover and simmer gently for about 15–20 minutes or until the water has been absorbed and rice is cooked.

Add the quorn, hard-boiled egg, parsley and cream (or fromage frais). Heat gently, stirring for 3–4 minutes. Serve immediately.

# HUNGARIAN LAMB

S E R V E S

—— 4 ——

This sweet-and-sour mince dish is delicious served with lightly boiled spring greens.

As everything is cooked in one pot there is very little washing-up involved in preparing this meal and the whole dish has a wonderful flavour. A trouble-free meal that can be left to cook on its own.

**Healthy Content:** *Carbohydrate, protein, iron, vitamins B and C. Some fat.*

---

Heat the oil in a large pan, add the onions and garlic and fry until the ingredients have softened. This should take about 5 minutes. Stir in the lamb and fry for a further 5 minutes. Drain off any excess fat.

Add the rice, red pepper, sultanas, dried herbs and paprika. Stir in the stock and soy sauce. Bring to the boil, cover and simmer for 15–20 minutes or until the rice is cooked. Serve immediately.

## INGREDIENTS

2 tablespoons sunflower oil
2 onions, peeled and
  chopped
1 clove garlic, peeled and
  crushed
350 g (12 oz) lean minced
  lamb
100 g (4 oz) easy cook
  wholegrain rice
1 red pepper, de-seeded and
  chopped
50 g (2 oz) sultanas
1 teaspoon dried mixed
  herbs
2 teaspoons paprika pepper
350 ml (12 fl oz) lamb
  stock
2 tablespoons rich soy sauce

# CHEESEY PASTA WITH CORN

### S E R V E S
### — 4 —

### INGREDIENTS

*225 g (8 oz) wholewheat pasta twists*
*2 teaspoons olive oil*
*275 g (10 oz) frozen sweetcorn, with peppers*

**FOR THE CHEESE SAUCE**
*40 g (1¹/₂ oz) polyunsaturated margarine*
*40 g (1¹/₂ oz) plain flour*
*600 ml (1 pint) semi-skimmed milk*
*2 teaspoons wholegrain mustard*
*Pinch of cayenne pepper*
*75 g (3 oz) mature Cheddar cheese, grated*

The wholemeal pasta gives a lovely nutty flavour to this creamy supper dish. 100 g (4 oz) of wholewheat pasta provides 10 g (¹/₄ oz) dietary fibre. This dish is best served with grilled tomatoes.

***Healthy Content:*** *High in carbohydrate, protein as well as B vitamins and calcium. Fibre. Some fat.*

Cook the pasta in a large pan of boiling water and the olive oil until just tender. For cooking time follow the directions on the packet – probably about 10–15 minutes. Stir once or twice to prevent sticking and add sweetcorn to pan for the last 5 minutes.

Meanwhile, make the sauce. Put all the ingredients, except the cheese, into a medium-sized pan. Heat gently, stirring until the margarine melts, then increase heat and stir until sauce boils and thickens. Then add the cheese and stir until it melts. Continue to cook gently for 5 minutes.

Drain pasta, top with sauce and serve immediately.

# THREE-GRAIN
# CE SALAD WITH MANGO

### SERVES
### — 4 —

The stark black grains of wild rice look dramatic in this delicious salad. Although wild rice is rather expensive, a little goes a long way and the effect is well worth it. This is a quick and easy recipe because all the grains can be cooked together in one pan whilst the mango and celery are being prepared and the dressing made.

Mangoes are exotic fruits now available in most supermarkets. Peel the mango and chop the flesh, discarding the large central stone.

This salad will be the talking point of any dish you serve with it.

*Healthy Content: High in carbohydrate, fibre, vitamins A and C.*

Put the brown and wild rice into a large saucepan with 1 litre (2 pints) water. Bring to the boil, cover with a lid and simmer for about 30 minutes, or until rice is cooked and wild rice grains split open. Add the white rice for the last 12 minutes of the cooking time.

Meanwhile, prepare the dressing. Put all the ingredients into a mug and whisk with a fork.

Drain the rice in a sieve and, if serving cold, rinse with plenty of cold water, drain and turn into a large mixing bowl. Add the mint and the dressing, toss to combine and allow to cool completely. Add the mango and celery just before serving.

If serving hot, put the drained rice straight into a mixing bowl. Add the mint, mango, celery and the dressing. Toss to combine. Turn into serving dish and serve immediately.

### INGREDIENTS

*100 g (4 oz) brown rice*
*50 g (2 oz) wild rice*
*100 g (4 oz) long-grain white rice*
*2 tablespoons chopped fresh mint*
*1 ripe mango, peeled and diced*
*2 celery stalks, chopped*

**FOR THE DRESSING**
*2 tablespoons sunflower oil*
*Juice 1 lime*
*1 teaspoon fresh ginger, grated*
*2 teaspoons clear honey*
*Freshly ground black pepper*

# TORTELLINI VERDI
# WITH CARROT SAUCE

### SERVES
### —— 4 ——

**INGREDIENTS**

**FOR THE CARROT SAUCE**
*450 g (1 lb) carrots, peeled and diced*
*1 celery stalk, finely chopped*
*150 ml (5 fl oz) vegetable stock*
*3 parsley sprigs*
*150 ml (5 fl oz) pure orange juice*
*1 × 250 g (9 oz) packet Tortellini Verdi (with cheese filling)*

**TO SERVE**
*Fresh parsley, chopped*

This spinach pasta with a cheese filling is ideal for entertaining. It cooks quickly and has a fresh flavour. The carrot sauce is enhanced with orange juice and the colour is pretty against the green of the tortellini.

Complete the dish with a mixed salad which includes red and green peppers.

**Healthy Content:** *Lots of vitamin A from the carrots as well as protein, carbohydrate, fibre and vitamin C. Low in fat.*

First, prepare the carrot sauce. Put the carrots, celery, stock and parsley into a medium-sized saucepan. Cover and bring to the boil, then simmer for 12–15 minutes, until tender. Turn into food processor and process into a purée. Add the orange juice with 85 ml (3 fl oz) water. Process again.

Empty the tortellini into a large saucepan of boiling water, return to the boil and simmer for 12–13 minutes.

Meanwhile, return the carrot sauce to the pan and gently stir and re-heat. Drain the pasta, pour over the carrot sauce, sprinkle with the chopped parsley and serve immediately.

# QUICK PORK AND SPAGHETTI

**SERVES**

— 4 —

Lean high-protein cubed pork cooks very quickly. In this recipe the pork is extended with sweetcorn, peas and a tin of spaghetti in tomato sauce to make a quick family meal. Serve with bread or jacket potatoes.

**Healthy Content:** *High in carbohydrate, protein. Also B vitamins, vitamin C, iron, and a little fat.*

Heat the oil in a medium-sized saucepan. Add the pork and fry over a medium heat for 5 minutes, stirring frequently. Add the curry powder, stir well, then add the water with the sweetcorn and peas. Bring to the boil, cover and simmer for 5 minutes. Add the spaghetti and heat through gently, stirring constantly. Serve immediately.

### INGREDIENTS

*1 tablespoon corn oil*
*350 g (12 oz) lean pork fillet, cubed*
*1 teaspoon curry powder*
*85 ml (3 fl oz) water*
*100 g (4 oz) frozen sweetcorn kernels*
*100 g (4 oz) frozen peas*
*1 × 425 g (15 oz) can spaghetti in tomato sauce (reduced salt and sugar variety)*

# TUNA AND CRAB PASTA SAVOURY

### SERVES
— 4 —

This meal is cooked in one large saucepan so once again saves on the washing-up! A filling dish using mainly convenience foods.

An ideal special meal to serve for guests. To complete the meal, serve accompanied by crusty bread and a green salad.

***Healthy Content:*** *High in carbohydrate, protein, fibre, calcium and vitamins A and D. Some fat from the cream.*

---

Cook the pasta in a large pan of boiling water and the olive oil, until just tender. Follow the directions on the packet for cooking time, probably about 8–10 minutes. Add the frozen mixed vegetables in the last 5 minutes of the cooking time. Drain and return to the pan.

Meanwhile, combine the fromage frais, half cream, Worcestershire sauce and the tomato purée, stir and season with black pepper. Add to the pasta with the tuna and crabmeat and continue stirring. Heat gently, stirring for 3 or 4 minutes. Sprinkle with the parsley and serve immediately.

## INGREDIENTS

*275 g (10 oz) tricolour pasta twists*
*2 teaspoons olive oil*
*175 g (6 oz) frozen mixed vegetables (peas, beans, carrots and sweetcorn)*
*85 ml (3 fl oz) fromage frais*
*284 ml (10 fl oz) half cream*
*1/2 teaspoon Worcestershire sauce*
*2 teaspoons tomato purée*
*Freshly ground black pepper*
*1 × 200 g (7 oz) can tuna in water or brine, drained*
*1 × 170 g (5 1/2 oz) can white crabmeat, drained*

**TO SERVE**
*2 tablespoons fresh parsley, chopped*

# FETTUCCINE WITH ASPARAGUS SAUCE

### S E R V E S
### —— 4 ——

Either fettuccine or tagliatelle can be used in this recipe. Both are long strands of flat pasta, sold dried, in nest shapes. Fettuccine is a little narrower and thicker than tagliatelle. Select either the golden yellow variety which contains egg or the green kind (fettuccine verdi) which contains spinach.

This quickly-made, filling meal is particularly easy to put together from store-cupboard ingredients and tastes wonderful with a simple salad and a bottle of chilled Chablis on a summer's evening.

**Healthy Content:** *High in carbohydrate, with protein, calcium, fibre, iron, B vitamins, some fat.*

---

Cook the pasta in a large pan of boiling water and the olive oil until just tender. Follow the directions on the packet for cooking time, probably about 8–10 minutes.

Meanwhile make a one-step white wine sauce. Put the butter into a medium-sized pan, with the flour, milk, stock and white wine or cider. Heat slowly until the butter melts, then increase the heat and bring to the boil, stirring constantly. Simmer gently for 2 minutes and keep stirring until a creamy sauce results.

Add the ham and asparagus and heat through. Drain the pasta, top with the sauce and serve immediately.

### INGREDIENTS

*225 g (8 oz) fettuccine*
*2 teaspoons olive oil*
*25 g (1 oz) butter*
*40 g (1¹/₂ oz) plain wholemeal flour*
*150 ml (5 fl oz) semi-skimmed milk*
*250 ml (8 fl oz) chicken stock*
*3 tablespoons dry white wine or cider*
*100 g (4 oz) lean ham, cut into strips*
*1 × 340 g (12 oz) can asparagus, drained and chopped*

# PERFECT POULTRY

As well as being versatile and quick and easy to cook, poultry is also healthy with a high proportion of lean tissue and little fat, especially if you remove the skin. Of all poultry, turkey is the lowest in fat – 2.7 g per 100 g – and the fat it contains is high in unsaturated fatty acids.

In this section I have used a variety of healthy recipes for turkey, duck, chicken and chicken livers. Many of the recipes include a sauce and I have suggested quick and easy serving accompaniments. Several different cooking methods are used with quick and easy preparation and cooking very much in mind. One or two of the recipes require a marinade. This can always be done the night before, if you prefer, to save you time when you actually want to cook the meal fast.

Try Chicken Tikka (see p. 107), Turkey à l'Orange (see p. 99) or Sesame Duck with Redcurrant Sauce (see p. 108). All these recipes prove how easy it is to serve attractive poultry dishes that are quick and easy to make, yet taste wonderful.

# Turkey a l'Orange

**S E R V E S**

— 4 —

This easy recipe is quick to make, uses few ingredients, yet tastes wonderful. Try serving it for Sunday lunch instead of the traditional roast.

I buy turkey breasts frozen from the supermarket – it's always a good idea to keep a stock of them in the freezer.

***Healthy Content:*** *Protein, B vitamins. Olive oil is high in monounsaturates.*

---

Heat the oil in a large frying-pan. Sprinkle the turkey breasts with the tarragon and fry for 10–12 minutes, turning occasionally. Transfer to a serving dish and keep warm.

Add the lime juice and rind, marmalade, stock and arrowroot to the pan. Slowly bring to the boil, stirring constantly. Simmer for 1–2 minutes until the sauce thickens slightly.

Pour a little sauce over the turkey, sprinkle with the chives and serve immediately. The remaining sauce can be served as an optional extra separately.

**INGREDIENTS**

*2 tablespoons olive oil*
*4 skinned turkey breasts,*
*each weighing about*
*175 g (6 oz)*
*1 teaspoon dried tarragon*
*Juice and rind from 1 lime*
*3 tablespoons medium cut,*
*fresh orange marmalade*
*150 ml (5 fl oz) chicken or*
*turkey stock*
*2 teaspoons arrowroot*

**TO SERVE**
*A few snipped fresh chives*

# CREAMY CURRIED TURKEY

### SERVES
—— 4 ——

## INGREDIENTS

150 ml (5 fl oz) fromage
   frais
3 tablespoons semi-
   skimmed milk
2 tablespoons mayonnaise
   (reduced calorie)
1 tablespoon apricot jam
1 teaspoon lemon juice
Grated rind of ¹/₂ orange
1¹/₂ teaspoons curry powder
350 g (12 oz) cold cooked
   turkey breast, chopped
2 celery stalks, chopped
1 red pepper, de-seeded and
   chopped

### TO SERVE
2 Little Gem lettuces
1 orange, segmented

Cold cooked turkey in a creamy, lightly curry-flavoured low fat dressing. This is an attractive dish to serve on any summer's day or for a buffet. Serve on a bed of lettuce accompanied by wholemeal rolls or French bread.

**Healthy Content:** High in protein, and calcium. Low fat. Some fibre and vitamin C from the vegetables.

Put the fromage frais into a large mixing bowl. Add the milk, mayonnaise, apricot jam, lemon juice, orange rind and curry powder. Stir to blend well. Add the turkey, celery and red pepper. Stir until well mixed.

Arrange the lettuce around the edge of oval serving dish and decorate with the orange segments. Spoon the turkey mixture into centre and serve immediately.

# CRUNCHY
## CHICKEN LIVER SAVOURY

**S E R V E S**

—— 4 ——

This chicken liver mixture looks particularly attractive and is delicious with the cooked cabbage. The cabbage is super-quick to cook.

Serve with chunks of wholemeal bread to mop up the juices, or jacket potatoes.

**Healthy Content:** *Protein, iron, B vitamins, vitamin C and fibre. Polyunsaturated fat from the corn oil and seeds.*

---

Using a sharp knife, cut the cabbage into quarters and cut away the hard stalk, then shred the leaves finely by hand. Heat a wok or large frying-pan and dry-fry the sesame seeds for a few seconds, until toasted. Turn them in the pan as they toast and tip the seeds onto a plate.

Heat 2 tablespoons of the oil in the pan and stir-fry the bacon and chicken livers for about 5 minutes over a fairly high heat until bacon crisps and the livers brown. Transfer to a plate, using a draining spoon.

Add the remaining oil and cabbage to the pan. Stir-fry using two wooden spoons until the cabbage turns bright green and starts to soften a little. Add the stock, bring to the boil, stirring constantly. Simmer for 2 minutes. Add the chicken livers and bacon, sesame seeds and a seasoning of black pepper. Re-heat gently, stirring 1–2 minutes, then serve immediately.

**INGREDIENTS**

*750 g (1½ lb) summer cabbage*
*1 teaspoon sesame seeds*
*3 tablespoons corn oil*
*2 rashers lean back bacon, rinded and chopped*
*450 g (1 lb) chicken livers, trimmed and halved*
*85 ml (3 fl oz) vegetable stock*
*Freshly ground black pepper*

# SPICED CHICKEN SAUTE

### SERVES
### — 4 —

Serve this super-fast chicken dish with new potatoes. Try not to overcook the vegetables so as not to lose their food value or flavour. They should be tender but not soft. The small amount of single cream adds a touch of luxury and provides an almost instant sauce.

*Healthy Content: Protein, vitamin C, fibre and fat from the cream and the oil.*

**INGREDIENTS**

2 tablespoons corn oil
450 g (1 lb) skinned and
    boneless chicken breast
1 onion, peeled and
    chopped
100 g (4 oz) button
    mushrooms, sliced
100 g (4 oz) frozen green
    beans
1 tablespoon plain flour
1 teaspoon hot paprika
    pepper
150 ml (5 fl oz) chicken
    stock
Freshly ground black
    pepper
150 ml (5 fl oz) single
    cream
A few drops Worcestershire
    sauce

Heat the oil in a large frying-pan or wok. Slice the chicken into thin strips and stir-fry it over a fairly high heat for about 4 minutes until lightly browned. Lift out with a draining spoon, cover and keep warm.

Add the onion, mushrooms and beans to the pan. Stir-fry for about 5 minutes until the ingredients begin to soften. Mix in the flour and paprika and cook for a further minute. Stir in the stock. Season with a little black pepper. Bring to the boil, stirring. Add the chicken and cream to the pan. Simmer, covered for 5–6 minutes or until chicken and vegetables are cooked. Add Worcestershire sauce to taste.

Serve immediately.

SESAME DUCK WITH REDCURRANT SAUCE (*page 108*)

# CHILLI TURKEY

## SERVES

### — 4 —

Minced turkey is quick to cook and contains less fat than chicken. As chilli con carne is usually made with beef, this turkey version will make a refreshing change. Serve with a mixed salad. The Mexicans serve this dish with grated Cheddar and a little grated chocolate, but don't go their route which isn't particularly healthy. Instead serve it with a mixed salad.

If you're entertaining, a jug of Sangria goes very well with this meal.

**Healthy Content:** Carbohydrate, protein, fibre, vitamin C. Low fat.

---

Heat the oil in a medium-sized saucepan. Fry the onion and red pepper for 5 minutes. If you have access to a food processor you can mince the turkey breast yourself or, alternatively, buy it ready-minced at the supermarket. Once minced, add the turkey, chilli peppers, cinnamon and coriander. Fry for 4 minutes, stirring constantly. Add the tomatoes and tomato purée and season with a little salt. Cover and simmer for 20 minutes. Add the kidney beans and, still stirring, heat through thoroughly.

Serve immediately.

**INGREDIENTS**

1–2 tablespoons corn oil
1 onion, peeled and chopped
1 red pepper, de-seeded and chopped
450 g (1 lb) turkey breast, skinned and minced
$^1/_4$ teaspoon crushed chilli peppers
$^1/_2$ teaspoon cinnamon
1 teaspoon ground coriander
1 × 400 g (14 oz) can chopped tomatoes
2 tablespoons tomato purée
A little salt
1 × 440 g (15$^1/_2$ oz) can red kidney beans, rinsed and drained

SUMMER FRUIT SALAD (page 127)

# CHINESE CHICKEN

### S E R V E S

### —— 4 ——

*12 chicken thigh portions, skinned and boned*

**FOR THE MARINADE**

*2 tablespoons white wine vinegar*

*2 tablespoons soy sauce*

*5 tablespoons pineapple juice*

*3 teaspoons runny honey*

*ice*

*eeled and*

*E*
*E*

*arrowroot*

These crisp and tasty chicken portions are best marinated overnight in the piquant mixture. Then they are simply roasted in the oven and the marinade and chicken juices are used to make a sauce. I buy frozen chicken thighs, skinned and boned, and I make sure I've always got a bag in the freezer as a stand-by. An excellent quick and easy Sunday lunch.

Cook some jacket potatoes in the oven at the same time as the chicken, allowing a little longer for the potatoes, of course. A simple salad, prepared whilst the chicken cooks, completes this meal.

*Healthy Content: Protein, B vitamins, with some fat and carbohydrate.*

Without opening them out arrange the thigh portions in a shallow dish. Combine all the ingredients for the marinade and pour over the chicken. Cover and set aside for at least 1 hour, or refrigerate overnight. Turn the thigh portions in the marinade once or twice.

Pre-heat the oven to gas mark 7, 425°F (220°C). Lift out the chicken portions and place in a roasting tin. Leave the marinade to one side. Bake, towards the top of the oven for 40 minutes until well browned and tender, turning and basting occasionally. Towards the end of the cooking time, pour off the juices into a medium-sized saucepan. Blend the marinade and arrowroot together and add to the juices in the pan. Bring to the boil, stirring constantly, and simmer for 1–2 minutes.

Pour the sauce over the chicken and serve.

# CHICKEN TIKKA

**S E R V E S**

—— 4 ——

Healthy and easy to cook, chicken tikka is one of the most popular dishes served in Indian restaurants.

Make this quick version yourself and serve it on a bed of brown rice to which a little turmeric has been added to give it a pretty yellow colour and a true Indian flavour.

**Healthy Content:** *High in protein and low in fat, B vitamins. Some calcium from the yoghurt.*

Pre-heat the oven to gas mark 8, 450°F (230°C).

Put the yoghurt into a medium-sized mixing bowl. Add the lemon juice, paprika, chilli powder and garlic. Season with a little salt, and stir well.

Coat the chicken with the resulting mixture, cover and set aside for 30 minutes or refrigerate overnight.

Arrange the chicken breasts in a roasting tin. Sprinkle them with the oil and cook for about 35 minutes until well-charred on the outside, basting occasionally.

Serve immediately.

## INGREDIENTS

*150 ml (5 fl oz) low fat natural yoghurt*
*1 tablespoon lemon juice*
*2 teaspoons paprika pepper*
*2 teaspoons mild chilli powder*
*1 clove garlic, peeled and crushed*
*A little salt*
*4 part-boned chicken breasts, skinned*
*1 tablespoon corn oil*

# SESAME DUCK WITH REDCURRANT SAUCE

### S E R V E S

— 4 —

**INGREDIENTS**

*4 duckling breast portions, at room temperature*

*1 tablespoon clear honey*

*1–2 tablespoons sesame seeds*

**FOR THE REDCURRANT SAUCE**

*150 ml (5 fl oz) light chicken or vegetable stock*

*4 tablespoons red grape juice or red wine*

*1 teaspoon dried tarragon*

*100 g (4 oz) redcurrants fresh or frozen (remove stalks)*

*40 g (1¹/₂ oz) demerara sugar*

*1 tablespoon cornflour*

Duck breasts, flavoured with sesame seeds, bake to crisp perfection in just 30 minutes. The redcurrants provide a tangy contrast to the richness of the duck.

Most of the fat will run out of the duck as it roasts leaving moist portions, high in protein. Serve on a bed of steaming boiled rice mixed with 2 tablespoons chopped fresh parsley, adding colour and vitamin C. Accompany with sticks of fresh vegetables blanched for 2–3 minutes or garden peas.

*Healthy Content: Protein, vitamins, fibre, some fat and carbohydrate (sugars). Redcurrants are rich in vitamin C and sesame seeds are rich in calcium.*

Oil the grill rack and pre-heat the grill on a high temperature. Prick the skin of the duck all over to help release the fat and grill on both sides, turning the grill down to medium once the breasts have sealed. Continue to grill them until they are almost completely cooked, then brush skin all over with honey and sprinkle with sesame seeds. Place under the grill again until they are crisp and golden. Transfer to a serving dish and keep warm.

Meanwhile, prepare the sauce. Put stock, grape juice, tarragon, redcurrants and sugar into a saucepan and heat, stirring, for 3 minutes. Blend the cornflour with 2 tablespoons of water and stir into the sauce off the heat. Replace the pan on a medium heat and stir until the sauce boils and thickens.

To serve, arrange duck breasts whole or in slices on oval dish, spooning a little of the sauce over. Serve the remainder of the sauce separately.

# *F*ANNED DUCK BREASTS, PEKING-STYLE

### S E R V E S
#### —— 4 ——

These oriental duck breasts taste fantastic but thankfully they're lower in fat than you may think. 100 g (4 oz) of oven-cooked duck breasts contain 255 calories with 28.8 g of body-building protein and 15.5 g fat.

This Chinese style recipe is particularly tasty served with the accompanying apricot sauce and some fresh vegetables in season. Warm French bread will complete the meal.

***Healthy Content:*** *High protein, with some fat, sugars and fibre.*

Pre-heat the oven to gas mark 6, 400°F (200°C).

Mix the soy sauce and honey together. Score the skin of the duck breasts several times with a sharp knife. Brush duck breasts on both sides with the soy mixture and leave to stand for 15 minutes. Cook, uncovered in a roasting tin for 40–45 minutes basting once half-way through.

To make the sauce, drain the apricots from their juice. Put the apricot juice into a medium pan with the chicken or duck stock. Blend the cornflour with 2 tablespoons cold water to make a smooth paste and stir into the stock and fruit juice. Bring to the boil, stirring constantly. Simmer gently and continue to stir for 1–2 minutes, until the mixture thickens. Add the halved apricots. Re-heat gently without boiling.

To serve, cut the duck breasts into thin slices and fan out on a warmed serving dish. Spoon over a little of the sauce, serving the remainder separately.

**INGREDIENTS**

*2 tablespoons soy sauce*
*2 tablespoons clear honey*
*4 boneless duck breasts,*
  *each weighing 180–*
  *240 g (6–8 oz)*

**FOR THE SAUCE**
*1 × 411 g (14¹/₂ oz) can*
  *apricots, in natural juice*
*150 ml (5 fl oz) chicken or*
  *duck stock*
*1 tablespoon cornflour*

# LEMON POUSSIN

### SERVES

### — 4 —

**INGREDIENTS**

2 poussins (skinned,
    optional)
Grated rind and juice of 1¹/₂
    lemons
2 cloves garlic, peeled and
    crushed
3 tablespoons olive oil
1 tablespoon freshly
    chopped coriander or
    parsley

TO GARNISH
25 g (1 oz) butter
50 g (2 oz) flaked almonds
25 g (1 oz) sunflower seeds

TO SERVE
1 packet ready-prepared
    salad leaves

Marinated poussins can be cooked on the barbecue or quickly grilled. With a crisp garnish, these well flavoured poussins are lovely with a salad and some granary bread and make a main meal suitable for entertaining. A little butter is used in this recipe to perfect its superb flavour.

*Healthy Content: Protein, B vitamins, vitamin C, some fat from the oil, butter and the almonds. Sunflower seeds are rich in calcium.*

Halve the poussins and arrange them in a shallow dish. Combine the lemon rind and juice with the garlic and olive oil. Stir in the coriander, then pour over the poussins. Set aside for 15 minutes, turning the poussins in the marinade once or twice. Transfer to grill rack.

Cook the birds under a pre-heated medium-hot grill for 15 minutes on each side. Baste with the marinade and turn them over once or twice as they cook. You will know they are cooked when you pierce them with a sharp knife and the juices run clear.

Meanwhile, melt the butter in a frying-pan, add the almonds and sunflower seeds and sauté for 2–3 minutes until toasted. Drain on absorbent kitchen paper.

To prepare the salad turn the packet of salad leaves into a serving bowl, top with the nuts and seeds and serve immediately.

# Easy coq au vin

S E R V E S

—— 4 ——

This quick to make coq au vin tastes as good as the traditional version. It's healthier too as the chicken is grilled thus removing a good deal of the fat. Serve with boiled rice or salad and bread.

*Healthy Content: High in protein, B vitamins, some fibre from the vegetables and polyunsaturated fat from the oil.*

Arrange the chicken in a shallow dish. Combine the wine with the garlic, herbs and 2 tablespoons of the oil and pour over the chicken. Marinate for a minimum of 20 minutes or preferably overnight.

Lightly oil a grill rack, remove the chicken from marinade (put the marinade to one side) and cook under a medium-hot grill, for 20–30 minutes, turning occasionally, until cooked through.

Heat the remaining oil in a medium-sized saucepan, fry onions and bacon with the sugar for about 7–10 minutes until the onions are soft and golden. Blend the cornflour with the stock and add to the pan with the marinade and mushrooms. Bring to the boil, stirring constantly. Simmer for 3–4 minutes.

Arrange the chicken on serving dish, pour over the sauce and serve immediately.

## INGREDIENTS

1 × 1.5 kg (3 lb) fresh chicken divided into 8 pieces

450 ml (15 fl oz) red wine

1 clove garlic, peeled and chopped

1 teaspoon dried mixed herbs

3 tablespoons sunflower oil

6 small onions, peeled and quartered

3 slices lean streaky bacon, rinded and chopped

1 teaspoon demerara sugar

1 tablespoon cornflour

150 ml (5 fl oz) chicken stock

175 g (6 oz) button mushrooms, halved

TO SERVE

2 tablespoons fresh parsley, chopped

# CHICKEN KORMA

**SERVES**

— 4 —

**INGREDIENTS**

750 g (1¹/₂ lb) skinned,
   boneless chicken
4 tablespoons plain
   wholemeal flour
2 tablespoons curry powder
3 tablespoons corn oil
2 cloves garlic, peeled and
   crushed
¹/₂ teaspoon dried coriander
450 ml (15 fl oz) chicken
   stock
25 g (1 oz) raisins
2 teaspoons lemon juice
4 tablespoons low fat
   natural yoghurt
25 g (1 oz) flaked almonds
300 ml (10 fl oz) brown
   rice, cooked

This quick and easy curry cooks in about the same time as a pan of rice. The yoghurt and almonds add a touch of luxury and creaminess to this mild dish. Although almonds are high in fat, only 25 g (1 oz) are used and they do add an authentic flavour to the meal.

**Healthy Content:** *Protein, B vitamins. Carbohydrate and a little fibre in the rice. Calcium from the yoghurt. Low fat.*

Cut the chicken into large pieces and coat them in a mixture of the flour and curry powder. Heat the oil in a wok or large frying-pan, fry the garlic and coriander for about 10 seconds, then add in the chicken pieces. Stir over a medium heat until lightly browned on all sides. Add the stock, raisins and lemon juice and bring to the boil, stirring constantly. Cover and simmer for 20 minutes and remove from the heat. Stir in the yoghurt and almonds and re-heat gently, but do not boil.

Serve immediately on a bed of rice.

# SIMPLE DESSERTS AND
# EASY WHOLESOME BAKES

The quickest, healthiest dessert is without doubt a piece of fresh fruit. High in vitamins and fibre, yet low in calories, fresh fruit naturally cleanses the palate, so make sure you always have a bowl of fruit on the table. Don't think you must offer exotic varieties, seasonal British fruits are excellent.

As most people enjoy the pleasure of eating a dessert, I have compiled these speedy, healthy puddings and included some instant recipes which, like the instant starters, give quick, simple yet effective finales to any meal.

When you want to serve something with a dessert, avoid high fat products like cream. A little single cream is a delicious luxury but a bowl of fromage frais or natural yoghurt sweetened with a little runny honey is a healthy and tasty alternative. I use the reduced fat version of evaporated milk quite often too.

Home-made cakes and biscuits are always popular, so I've included one large cake and two cookie recipes. The Surprise Slice (see p. 115) is wonderfully moist and made with carrots, wholewheat flour and chopped walnuts; it's high in fibre too. Speedy Spicy Oatcakes (see p. 125) are equally welcome with a cup of tea or coffee, or as an accompaniment to cheese and fruit as a quick lunch or supper. The Crunchy Peanut and Raisin Cookies (see p. 124) will be especially popular with the children.

## INSTANT DESSERTS

● Pour a small carton of natural yoghurt into a cereal bowl. Add 25 g (1 oz) seedless raisins and 1 small Cox's apple, cored and chopped. Sprinkle a teaspoonful of runny honey over the lot and serve immediately.

● Half fill ramekin dishes with stewed apples, hot or cold. Top with a crunchy breakfast cereal and serve immediately with natural yoghurt or low fat evaporated milk.

• Keep a stock of pancakes in the freezer, they defrost quickly and can be served filled with stewed fruit or natural yoghurt and sliced banana.

• Serve half a diced mango per person in a dessert bowl with a dash of Grand Marnier poured over and a spoonful of fromage frais or Greek yoghurt.

• For an instant fruit salad, turn a can of pineapple pieces in natural juice into a serving bowl. Add a few hulled sliced strawberries and a sliced banana. Serve immediately with low fat evaporated milk or single cream.

• Purée some drained peaches, canned in natural juice, in a food processor. Layer the purée into wine glasses with crushed ginger biscuits mixed with a few toasted almonds. Serve immediately.

• Serve hot toasted crumpets, spread with a fruit conserve, topped with a spoonful of fromage frais.

• Ice-cream and sorbets kept in the freezer are instant dessert stand-bys. If you buy ready-made varieties, read the contents labels carefully and choose the low sugar and low fat varieties. Ice-cream is a good source of calcium and 3 scoops of vanilla ice-cream contain only about 130 calories.

## QUICK TIPS

• Mix fromage frais or natural yoghurt with puréed fruits for a quick and easy fruit fool.

• Dissolve jellies in a measuring jug in the microwave with 150 ml (5 fl oz) water for 1½ minutes. Stir in cold water, up to 600 ml (1 pint) and 3 sliced bananas. Set in the refrigerator.

• Citrus fruits yield far more juice if you pop them in the microwave. Two fruits need approximately 45 seconds.

• Dried fruit salad can be cooked in about 10 minutes so keep some in the cupboard as a convenient stand-by.

• Frozen raspberries and redcurrants add a splash of colour and plenty of fibre to fresh fruit salads.

# SURPRISE SLICE

**MAKES**

—— 1 kg (2 lb) cake ——

Although this cake takes nearly an hour to bake it is quick and easy to prepare and you can always buy ready-grated carrots from the supermarket if you don't want the bother of grating them.

A filling cake which can be served either as a dessert or tea time treat. The carrots give a moist texture to the cake and are the surprise ingredient.

***Healthy Content:*** *Carbohydrate, fibre, iron, protein and B vitamins from the flour and oats. Vitamin A from the carrots. Polyunsaturated fat from the corn oil.*

---

Pre-heat the oven to gas mark 4, 350°F (180°C).

Mix all the ingredients in a large mixing bowl with a wooden spoon until they combine. Turn the mixture into the tin and bake in the centre of the oven for 50 minutes–1 hour or until a skewer inserted in the centre comes out clean.

Leave to cool in the tin, then turn out onto a wire cooling rack and leave until cold. Serve in slices with natural yoghurt, if desired.

**INGREDIENTS**

*175 g (6 oz) superfine self-raising wholemeal flour*
*75 g (3 oz) porridge oats*
*100 g (4 oz) raisins*
*75 g (3 oz) walnuts, chopped*
*225 g (8 oz) carrots, scrubbed clean and grated*
*3 eggs, beaten with 175 ml (6 fl oz) corn oil*
*75 g (3 oz) soft brown sugar*
*You will need a 9 × 5 in (25 × 13 cm) loaf tin with the base greased and lined*

# CASHEW NUT TRIANGLES

**M A K E S**

—— 16 biscuits ——

INGREDIENTS

100 g (4 oz)
  polyunsaturated
  margarine
50 g (2 oz) demerara sugar
5 tablespoons clear honey
275 g (10 oz) rolled oats
1 tablespoon bran
¹/₂ teaspoon mixed spice
75 g (3 oz) cashew nuts,
  roughly chopped

These flapjacks are reasonably high in fibre, especially with the added bran. The cashew nuts are crisp and simply delicious! These biscuits keep well in an airtight tin and are ideal to take on picnics or to pop into the children's lunch boxes. Adults will enjoy them with a cup of tea.

*Healthy Content:* *Oats supply useful carbohydrate, fibre, fat, protein, and B vitamins. Nuts supply protein, fibre and vitamins. Some fats and sugars.*

Pre-heat the oven to gas mark 4, 350°F (180°C).

Grease and line the base of 2 × 18 cm (7 in) round sandwich tins. Slowly melt the margarine, sugar and honey in a large saucepan, stirring occasionally. Stir in the oats, bran, spice and nuts. Mix well. Divide the mixture between the prepared tins and spread evenly over the base. Press down well with the back of a metal spoon.

Bake for 25 minutes. Mark each round into 8 triangles. Leave to cool in the tin, then ease out and store in an airtight container.

★ The most time consuming part of this recipe is chopping the nuts, so although the flavour of the cashews is particularly good with the honey, try chopped walnuts or flaked almonds, which you can buy ready-prepared if you are in a desperate hurry.

# APPLE CRUMBLE

### S E R V E S
#### — 4 —

A crumble quickly turns stewed fruit into a filling family pudding that everyone enjoys. Serve this high fibre dessert with fromage frais or custard made with semi-skimmed milk and half the usual amount of sugar. Vary the fruit by trying plums with cinnamon, pears with a little crystallised ginger and apples with redcurrants or raspberries. A lovely hot finale to any meal.

*Healthy Content: High in fibre and carbohydrate. B vitamins and some polyunsaturated fat from the seeds and oil.*

━━━━━━

Pre-heat the oven to gas mark 5, 375°F (190°C).

Peel, core and slice the apples and put into the base of an ovenproof dish. Add the mincemeat and apple juice and mix together thoroughly.

Put the flour and oats into a mixing bowl. Add the oil and mix with a fork to distribute the ingredients evenly. Add the sugar and sunflower seeds. Spoon mixture over the apples.

Bake for 30–35 minutes. Serve immediately.

### INGREDIENTS

*675 g (1¹/₂ lb) apples, use
1 Bramley and make the
weight up with
Worcesters or Cox's*
*2 tablespoons sweet
mincemeat*
*2 tablespoons pure apple
juice or water*

**FOR THE CRUMBLE TOPPING**
*75 g (3 oz) wholemeal
flour*
*50 g (2 oz) porridge oats*
*3 tablespoons walnut oil*
*25 g (1 oz) demerara sugar*
*25 g (1 oz) honey-roasted
sunflower seeds*

# HONEY AND STRAWBERRY CLOUDS

### SERVES
### — 4 —

## INGREDIENTS

*400 ml (14 fl oz) fromage frais, chilled*
*2 tablespoons clear honey*
*225 g (8 oz) strawberries, hulled and roughly chopped*

**TO DECORATE**
*4 whole strawberries*
*4 wafers*

This simple dessert will be popular with all the family. 100 g (4 oz) of fromage frais contains only 50 calories, with less than 0.3 g fat, 8.0 g protein and 4.0 g carbohydrate. The strawberries provide a wonderful fresh flavour.

***Healthy Content:*** *High in protein, calcium, fibre and vitamin C.*

Turn the fromage frais into a mixing bowl. Blend in the honey, then fold in the prepared strawberries. Divide the mixture between 4 sundae dishes. Top each dish with a strawberry and decorate with a wafer.

Serve immediately.

# CREPES
## SUZETTE

### SERVES
#### — 4 —

Thin pancakes made with equal quantities of wholemeal and plain flour make a valuable contribution to any meal. A small amount of butter is used in the sauce to add to its superb flavour.

Serve these orange-flavoured pancakes on their own or with natural yoghurt.

**Healthy Content:** *Carbohydrate, fibre, protein, calcium, fat, B vitamins in the flour. Vitamin C in the orange segments.*

To prepare the batter, put the flour, egg and half the milk into a food processor and process until smooth, then add the remaining milk and process for a few extra seconds. Turn into a jug and allow to stand for 10 minutes.

To make the sauce, put the butter, sugar and grated rind and juice from 1 orange into a saucepan. Heat gently and stir until the butter melts and sugar dissolves, then bring to the boil and simmer for 2–3 minutes. Add the fresh orange segments and Cointreau and set aside.

Stir the batter, then make 8 pancakes in a small pan in a little hot oil, turning each pancake once, until golden. Fold each pancake in half and half again to form a triangle. Keep warm.

Overlap pancakes on serving dish. If necessary re-heat sauce, then pour over the pancakes. Serve immediately.

### INGREDIENTS

**FOR THE PANCAKES**
*50 g (2 oz) plain flour*
*50 g (2 oz) plain wholemeal flour*
*1 egg*
*300 ml (10 fl oz) semi-skimmed milk*

**FOR THE SAUCE**
*50 g (2 oz) butter*
*50 g (2 oz) caster sugar*
*Grated rind and juice of 1 orange*
*2 oranges, segmented*
*2 tablespoons Cointreau, optional*

# BLUE CHEESE
# WHOLEWHEAT SCONES

## MAKES
—— 8 scones ——

75 g (3 oz) self-raising
   wholemeal flour
75 g (3 oz) self-raising
   white flour
1 teaspoon baking powder
Pinch cayenne pepper
25 g (1 oz) butter
75 g (3 oz) blue Cheshire
   cheese, grated
1 tablespoon fresh chives,
   chopped
1 egg
4 tablespoons semi-
   skimmed milk

These delicious savoury scones are wonderful stand-bys as they freeze well. Serve them spread with a little low fat spread. The combination of the cheese and chives enhances the herb flavour of the scones.

They are ideal, warmed, at tea time or with a ploughman's lunch and excellent served with a bowl of home-made soup.

**Healthy Content:** *Carbohydrate, fibre and protein, some fat, B vitamins and calcium.*

Pre-heat oven to gas mark 7, 425°F (220°C).

Sift the flour into a bowl, adding any bran residue left in the sieve. Add the baking powder and pepper, then rub in the butter until mixture becomes crumbly.

Fork in the grated cheese with the chives. Beat the egg and 3 tablespoons of the milk together and mix into the flour to form a soft dough. Knead the dough and roll out to a thickness of about 1.5 cm (³/₄ in). Make sure you roll the dough to the right thickness. People often make the mistake of rolling it too thin and end up with biscuit-like scones! Using a cutter, cut out the scones and arrange on a baking sheet. Brush the surface of each scone with the remaining milk. Bake near the top of the oven for 15–20 minutes, until golden.

Serve warm or cold.

# *A*PPLE AND GOOSEBERRY SURPRISE

### S E R V E S
—— 4 ——

*A*ny crushed soft fruit can be used to make a fool, but gooseberries give the best flavour and texture of all the summer fruits. They are also high in fibre. Greek yoghurt is used instead of double cream and is delicious in this recipe, but it does contain 10 per cent animal fat. Gooseberries and Bramleys will vary in their sweetness, so be ready to alter the amount of sugar to taste.

Serve the dessert in wine glasses with almond wafers or digestive biscuits. This dessert is also good layered with a crunchy breakfast cereal.

*Healthy Content: Plenty of fibre and vitamin C. Also protein, calcium, some fat from the yoghurt.*

### INGREDIENTS

*450 g (1 lb) gooseberries, topped and tailed* **or**
*750 g (1½ lb) Bramley apples, peeled, cored and sliced*
*50 g (2 oz) caster sugar*
*About ¾ of a 200 g (7 oz) carton of Greek natural yoghurt*

**TO DECORATE**
*Tiny sprigs of fresh mint*

Put the gooseberries or apples into a large pan with 4 tablespoons of cold water. Cover and cook gently for about 15 minutes or until fruit has softened or, if you have a microwave, cook the fruit with the water, covered, in a large container for approximately 7 minutes. Allow to stand for 5 minutes.

Crush the fruit with the back of a wooden spoon, then mash to a purée with a fork – don't use a food processor or try to sieve the fruit; it should have a bit of texture. Add sugar to taste. Cool completely.

Empty the yoghurt into a mixing bowl and blend in the cool fruit purée. Add a little more sugar to taste.

Turn into wine glasses and chill for 1 hour. Serve decorated with the sprigs of mint.

# SPECTACULAR
## PINEAPPLE PEACHES

### SERVES

— 4 —

**INGREDIENTS**

*2 large ripe peaches*
*165 g (6 oz) quark low fat*
*   soft cheese*
**or** *165 g (6 oz) reduced fat*
*   cream cheese*
*1 × 225 g (8 oz) can*
*   pineapple slices in*
*   natural juice, drained*
*15–25 g ($^1/_2$–1 oz) icing*
*   sugar, sieved*

**TO DECORATE**

*A little ground cinnamon*
*   or ginger*

This dessert consists of peaches filled with a delicious low fat cream cheese and pineapple mixture, topped with cinnamon or ginger.

Quick to prepare, it will be particularly popular on a summer's evening. The pineapple adds fibre and a tangy, sherbet flavour.

***Healthy Content:*** *Fibre, protein, calcium and some vitamin A. Some fat and sugar.*

Halve the peaches, remove the stones and arrange the halves on 4 serving plates, with the hollow sides visible. Turn the quark or the reduced fat cream cheese into a mixing bowl. Add the chopped pineapple with 2 tablespoons of the reserved juice and the icing sugar. Stir until well mixed.

Pile the mixture into the hollows of the peaches and chill. Just before serving sprinkle each peach with the cinnamon or ginger.

★ Use canned peaches in natural juice when fresh ones are not available.

# SHERRIED BANANA BRULEE

### SERVES
—— 4 ——

Creamy brûlée with a crunchy caramelised topping is traditionally made from whipped double cream. This healthy version tastes just as good but is made with natural yoghurt and low fat fromage frais. Bananas are high in fibre and one banana provides about half the daily requirement of vitamin C.

*Healthy Content:* *Carbohydrate, fibre, potassium, calcium, protein.*

———

Divide the banana slices and the raisins between 4 ramekin dishes. Pour the sherry over each one evenly. Blend the fromage frais and the yoghurt together, then divide it between the ramekins, covering the bananas completely. Combine the sugar and cinnamon and sprinkle over the fromage frais mixture.

Put ramekins under a hot grill for a short time to caramelise the sugar. Chill for at least 20 minutes before serving.

**INGREDIENTS**

*2 bananas, sliced*
*50 g (2 oz) raisins*
*2 tablespoons medium sherry*
*12 tablespoons fromage frais*
*4 tablespoons natural low fat yoghurt*
*4 teaspoons demerara sugar*
*$^{1}/_{2}$ teaspoon cinnamon*

# CRUNCHY PEANUT AND RAISIN COOKIES

M A K E S

—— 14 cookies ——

These rough textured cookies are popular with children and will make a valuable contribution to their lunch boxes. These are low sugar cookies which are simple and convenient to make from store-cupboard ingredients.

**Healthy Content:** *Carbohydrate, protein, fibre, polyunsaturated fat, iron, B vitamins.*

### INGREDIENTS

*50 g (2 oz) crunchy peanut butter*
*50 g (2 oz) polyunsaturated margarine*
*50 g (2 oz) soft brown sugar*
*1 egg*
*100 g (4 oz) self-raising wholemeal flour*
*50 g (2 oz) raisins*
*25 g (1 oz) porridge oats*
*1 teaspoon mixed spice*

Pre-heat oven to gas mark 4, 350°F (180°C).

Cream together the peanut butter, margarine and sugar. Beat in the egg, then fold in the flour, raisins, oats and spice. Mix well to form a soft dough.

Divide dough into 14 even-sized pieces and roll into small balls. Space out on un-greased baking sheet. Flatten each cookie slightly with the prongs of a fork, leaving a slight indent.

Bake for 15–20 minutes until lightly golden. Allow to cool slightly on a baking sheet, then transfer to cooling rack.

Store in an airtight container.

# SPEEDY
## SPICY OATCAKES

**M A K E S**

—— approx. 12 biscuits ——

In this recipe the cooking oil and milk mix with the dry ingredients quickly and easily and there's no rolling out involved. These biscuits are a good source of fibre, but they are fairly high in fat so don't eat too many at once.

**Healthy Content:** *Carbohydrate, fibre, polyunsaturated fat, protein.*

---

Pre-heat the oven to gas mark 5, 375°F (190°C).

Sieve the flour, mixed spice and baking powder into a mixing bowl. Fork in the sugar and oats. Using a wooden spoon, mix in the oil and milk and bind the ingredients together. Roll the mixture into balls about the size of a walnut with your hands and place on a lightly greased baking sheet. Press down lightly with back of a spoon. Bake for approximately 15 minutes. Allow to cool. Store in an airtight container.

**INGREDIENTS**

*225 g (8 oz) plain wholemeal flour*
*2 teaspoons mixed spice*
*1 teaspoon baking powder*
*50 g (2 oz) light soft brown sugar*
*50 g (2 oz) porridge oats*
*120 ml (4 fl oz) sunflower oil*
*Approximately 4 tablespoons semi-skimmed milk*

# LEMON AND STRAWBERRY CHEESECAKE

**M A K E S**

—— 1 × 20 cm (8 in) cheesecake ——

## INGREDIENTS

75 g (3 oz)
  polyunsaturated
  margarine
150 g (5 oz) digestive
  biscuits, crushed
25 g (1 oz) honey-roasted
  sunflower seeds
1 lemon jelly tablet
175 g (6 oz) reduced-fat
  cream cheese
**or** 175 g (6 oz) cottage
  cheese, processed until
  smooth in food processor
50 g (2 oz) caster sugar
Grated rind and juice of 1
  lemon
350 ml (12 fl oz)
  evaporated milk, chilled
  for at least 2 hours

TO DECORATE
Sliced strawberries
You will need a 20 cm (8
  in) loose-bottomed cake
  tin

This healthy cheesecake is just as delicious as one made with double cream and full fat cream cheese, yet it's far lighter.

Using a jelly tablet instead of gelatine to set the cheesecake is quick and easy. The fruit decoration adds fibre and vitamin C to this dessert, which will freeze well.

***Healthy Content:*** *Carbohydrate, calcium, protein, some fat, vitamins A and D.*

Melt the margarine in a medium-sized saucepan. Stir in the crushed biscuits with the sunflower seeds. Mix well. Lightly grease the cake tin and press the mixture into the base.

Dissolve the jelly tablet in 150 ml (5 fl oz) water. Set aside to cool.

In a mixing bowl whisk together the cream cheese, sugar and the grated rind and juice from the lemon until light and fluffy. In a separate large bowl whip the evaporated milk until thick, then add the cream cheese mixture to it and whisk again to combine. Gradually whisk in the jelly.

Pour the mixture onto the biscuit base and chill to set. Just before serving decorate with sliced strawberries.

# SUMMER

## FRUIT SALAD

### S E R V E S

#### — 4 —

A few varieties of red fruits mixed with fresh orange juice and Kirsch tastes and looks fresh and summery served in glass sundae dishes or on white plates.

Use low fat fromage frais sweetened with a little honey as an accompaniment – it is lighter than whipped cream and just as delicious.

***Healthy Content:*** *High in fibre, vitamin C. The fromage frais is high in calcium and protein.*

Halve the strawberries and place into a large glass fruit bowl. Add the redcurrants. I used frozen redcurrants for this recipe as they are so easy to remove from the stalks when frozen. Put them in with the other fruits still frozen, they'll thaw rapidly. Add the diced nectarine. Mix the orange juice and Kirsch and pour over the fruits. Cover and chill for 20 minutes.

Stir the honey into the fromage frais. Serve the fruit and fromage frais in separate bowls.

### INGREDIENTS

*225 g (8 oz) strawberries, hulled*
*100 g (4 oz) redcurrants, removed from stalks*
*1 nectarine, diced*
*6 tablespoons pure orange juice*
*2 tablespoons Kirsch*

**FOR THE TOPPING**
*Clear honey, to taste*
*150 ml (5 fl oz) fromage frais*

**127**

# TEN DAILY MENUS

The following menus will help you put together complete meals by combining the recipes from this book.

On each of the ten days, choose one of the following quick and easy healthy breakfasts:

• Bran-based cereal served with sliced banana and semi-skimmed milk.

• Toasted wholemeal bread with low fat spread or polyunsaturated margarine topped with honey, marmalade or yeast extract. Offer fresh fruit in season.

• Porridge made with semi-skimmed milk and water. Add a handful of raisins on serving and low fat evaporated or semi-skimmed milk.

• Grill rashers of lean, fat-trimmed back bacon. Serve 2 per person with grilled tomatoes and wholemeal toast.

• Natural yoghurt with sliced banana, topped with sunflower seeds or chopped nuts.

# *F*AMILY MEAL

LUNCH
Chicken Korma (see p. 112)
Brown rice (see p. 83)
Pink and Green Coleslaw (see p. 56)

Honey and Strawberry Clouds (see p. 118)

SUPPER
Crab and Corn Chowder (see p. 22)
Wholemeal bread

Fresh fruit

# *M*IDSUMMER'S DAY

LUNCH
Creamy Curried Turkey (see p. 100)
Sweet-and-Sour Fennel and Grape Salad (see p. 52)
Mixed breads (wholemeal, pitta, rye or poppy-seed rolls)

Spectacular Pineapple Peaches (see p. 122)

ıce (see p. 97)
(see p. 47)

Sherried Banana Brûlée (see p. 123)

# *I*TALIAN DAY

### LUNCH

Tortellini Verdi with Carrot Sauce (see p. 94)
French bread, warmed
Sunshine Vegetables (see p. 48)

Fresh fruit

### SUPPER

Perfect Pizza Pie (see p. 80)
Pink and Green Coleslaw (see p. 56)

Spectacular Pineapple Peaches (see p. 122)

# *A* CELEBRATION

### LUNCH

Pan-Fried Trout with Orange (see p. 31)
Crunchy Vegetable Stir-Fry (see p. 47)
New potatoes

Lemon and Strawberry Cheesecake (see p. 126)

### SUPPER

Spiced Chicken Sauté (see p. 102)
Saucy Mediterranean Vegetables (see p. 53)

Bowl of fresh plums

# LAZY DAY

**LUNCH**

Chinese Chicken served cold (see p. 106)
Spicy Dhal served cold (see p. 54)
Pink and Green Coleslaw (see p. 56)

Surprise Slice (see p. 115) with Greek yoghurt

**SUPPER**

Five-Minute Chicken Broth made day before and re-heated (see p. 21)
Blue Cheese Wholewheat Scones from freezer, de-frosted (see p. 120)

# MOTHERS' DAY

**LUNCH**

Tuna and Crab Pasta Savoury (see p. 96)
Summer Salad (see p. 50)
Bread rolls

Summer Fruit Salad (see p. 127)

**SUPPER**

Perfect Florentine Pizzas (see p. 74)

Fresh fruit

# ORIENTAL DAY

**LUNCH**

Prawns and Peppers in Cider (see p. 40)
Three-Grain Rice Salad with Mango (see p. 93)
Wholemeal bread

Pineapple Fruit Salad (see p. 114)

**SUPPER**

Pork and Cashew Stir-Fry (see p. 77) with Vegetarian
Rice (see p. 86)
Summer salad (see p. 50)

Fresh fruit

# BOXING DAY

**LUNCH**

Creamy Cannellini Pâté (see p. 19)
Vegetarian Rice (see p. 86)
or
Creamy Curried Turkey (see p. 100)
Christmas Salad (see p. 46)
Bread rolls

Crêpes Suzette (see p. 119)
or
Apple Crumble (see p. 117)

**SUPPER**

Glazed Lamb with Soy Mushrooms (see p. 78)
Sunshine Vegetables (see p. 48)
Wholemeal bread rolls

Banana-filled Pancakes (see p. 114)

# HUNGRY TEENAGERS' DAY

**LUNCH**

Chicken Liver Savouries (see p. 19)
Jacket potatoes

Yoghurt with Apple (see p. 113)

**SUPPER**

Cheesey Pasta with Corn (see p. 92)
Vegetable Crumble (see p. 51)

Fresh fruit

# ENTERTAINING DAY

**LUNCH**

Ham and Egg Smash (see p. 63)
Cheesey Rice Tomatoes (see p. 24)

Surprise Slice (see p. 115)

**SUPPER**

Pea and Asparagus Soup (see p. 23)
Rump Steak with Cranberry Sauce (see p. 64)
Crunchy Vegetable Stir-Fry (see p. 47)
New potatoes

Honey and Strawberry Clouds (see p. 118)

# INDEX